THE HEART OF A DISCIPLE

Robert J. McCarty, DMin

Paulist Press
New York / Mahwah, NJ

Cover image by ARFGRPCH / Shutterstock.com
Cover design by Joe Gallagher
Book design by Lynn Else

Library of Congress Control Number: 2023938481

ISBN 978-0-8091-5678-8 (paperback)
ISBN 978-0-8091-8841-3 (e-book)

Published by Paulist Press
997 Macarthur Boulevard
Mahwah, New Jersey 07430

www.paulistpress.com

Printed and bound in the
United States of America

Acknowledgments

Many of the chapter themes in this book were developed for retreats given with my wife, Maggie McCarty. Maggie's insights were invaluable in translating my musings and ramblings into words.

I also benefitted greatly from the guidance, vision, and encouragement provided by Denise Anderson who served as my personal editor, created the chapter format, shaped the content, and wrote prayers for each chapter.

Finally, I am indebted to the countless pastoral ministers, teachers, and colleagues who have influenced and formed my thinking over the years. The ideas I present are a synthesis of all I have absorbed from you. Thank you.

Contents

Acknowledgments iii

Foreword by Mike Patin vii

Introduction 1

CHAPTER 1: A Disciple's Heart 5

CHAPTER 2: A Path with Heart 13

CHAPTER 3: A Heart for Ministry 21

CHAPTER 4: A Transcendent Heart 29

CHAPTER 5: The Dream of the Heart 35

CHAPTER 6: A Catholic Heart 41

CHAPTER 7: A Faithful Heart 49

CHAPTER 8: A Healing Heart 55

CHAPTER 9: Sharing Your Heart 63

CHAPTER 10: A Steadfast Heart 69

CHAPTER 11: Holy Hearts 75

CHAPTER 12: Hearts on Fire 83

CHAPTER 13: Following Your Heart 91

CHAPTER 14: A Liminal Heart 99

CHAPTER 15: My Heart 107

Foreword

I'm excited that Bob McCarty has shared his gifts and his reflections on discipleship in his book *The Heart of a Disciple*. I have known Bob for more than thirty years as we have worked together in various roles and capacities, primarily centered around Catholic youth ministry. When I became director of the Youth Ministry Office for the Archdiocese of New Orleans in 1994, Bob was in the Office of Youth Ministry for the Archdiocese of Baltimore, prior to serving as executive director of the National Federation for Catholic Youth Ministry (NFCYM) in Washington, DC. I wanted to learn about the nuts and bolts of youth work from him and his coworkers, so I traveled to their office for my personally designed in-service day. I listened to their vision and learned about best practices in programming and ministry management skills, but I received so much more: clarity, support, inspiration, and encouragement. Since that visit, these gifts have remained a blessing as I continue to benefit from my professional and personal relationship with Bob, as friends and colleagues in pastoral ministry.

One of the powerful metaphors in *The Heart of a Disciple* is the difference between a tourist on a trip and a pilgrim on a journey. While I might have been more of a tourist taking a trip when I first traveled to learn more about youth ministry, I became a pilgrim on a journey that has become more focused on discipleship. As I began reading this book, I found myself remembering the valuable gifts I had received from Bob. I already know I will revisit these pages to continue to gain insights into myself, my ministry, and my relationship with God. I pray the same for you.

My hope is that this book will become a valuable resource for the journeys and pilgrimages for all who encounter it. Bob is skilled at making connections in person and through his writing. He weaves together metaphor, story, wit, and the occasional bad pun to put words to our experiences and help us to discover grace within and around us. This book uses the language of faith to illumine the heart of discipleship. I find Bob to be prophetic as he names challenging realities of ministry and everyday life while he continues to remind us of our source of power and hope. Bob always points ahead, or to use one of his favorite words, "onward!"

I often ask Church leaders to reflect on the Mount Rushmore of their ministry and name the people who have most influenced their ways of thinking and approaches to ministry. Bob is on my Mount Rushmore. He has helped me and countless teens and adults by modeling what it means to be present, pastoral, and prophetic. He lives the virtues Pope Francis names in *The Joy of the Gospel*: encounter, dialogue, and accompaniment. Bob meets us where we are, listens carefully to what is said, and helps us break open our lives through thought-provoking and sometimes uncomfortable questions. He invites us to think slowly, attentively, and deeply. His ability to promote focused reflection has been a gift to many and can now be shared with those who read *The Heart of a Disciple*, with its invitation to look more closely at our lives, our faith, and our call to service.

There have been numerous times when Bob and I were both presenting workshops or keynote addresses at a conference and I would marvel at Bob's ability to evoke responses from a group, honor diverse experiences, and get to the heart of a topic with skill and ease. I always leave his presentations, and even our informal conversations, with much food for thought. These chapters do the same.

If we allow ourselves to break open our lives through intentional reflection and be guided by *The Heart of a Disciple*, we will find clarity, support, inspiration, and encouragement, just as I did in my beginning conversations with Bob more than three decades ago and in our shared ministry and friendship these many years since.

The disillusionment of the disciples who encountered Jesus on their journey to Emmaus in Luke 24:13–34 became a pilgrimage of self-reflection, faith conversation, grace-filled moments, and restored hope. The disciples' hearts burned within them as Jesus accompanied them on the road. *The Heart of a Disciple* expands our understanding of companions on the road, our ability to find our way forward, and our capacity to listen. Our hearts burn within us, over and over again. May your journey, pilgrimage, and heart be blessed!

Mike Patin
Catholic Speaker and Faith Horticulturist

Introduction

Why This Book

I am often asked to write book reviews for various publishing companies and encounter many advertisements about titles on spirituality, our spiritual journey, spiritual founders in our tradition, prayer, and a host of related topics. I always marvel at the breadth of authors' experiences and the variety of perspectives they bring to the quest for meaning, purpose, understanding, and holiness. But just when I think, "This book really captures the mystery," I find I am wrong. The mystery, the holy, God, or however we name the end of our quest, most often lies just beyond our reach, eluding our understanding, and especially our words. While each book can illumine a part of the mystery, I have found none that captures the entire reality.

And so, we travel together—as readers, pilgrims, and an author serving as guide on this shared stretch of the road on our human journey. At any given moment, both readers and authors share experience, insight, and knowledge that influence what we speak, hear, write, and understand—and somehow a connection. What a wonderful grace and mystery!

I have come to believe *we are experience rich and language poor*. We bring our whole lives to any learning opportunity, but we often don't have language to share our experience with others, or even have the words to understand it more completely ourselves. I believe the best learning opportunities help us find words to appreciate and share our lives. Likewise, the best teachers, professors, spiritual directors, pastoral leaders, and authors provide a vocabulary that helps us speak to our experience. This is especially important when it comes to sharing our encounters with God, since God is beyond words. In the Christian Scriptures, we have four Gospels; yet even these four perspectives, from those who were closest to Jesus, offer only a glimpse of what centuries of believers have tried to express about resurrection and discipleship.

Why Write

Why did the disciples take the time to write it all down? Why did they keep track of the letters they wrote to Christian communities about how to live their post-Jesus lives? We don't know why exactly, but their questions, answers, insights, perspectives, and struggles still resonate in the hearts of faithful churchgoers, who listen to the same Scriptures every Sunday for three years and then start all over again. We continue to learn from past disciples—their experiences, fallibilities, feelings, hopes, and even their arrogance. And we still learn from each other. That is perhaps how authors come to be. We write down our experiences, thoughts, and insights, and hope they might be helpful to others.

I write from the perspective of my life and ministry. I am a husband, father, and grandfather. I am formed in the Roman Catholic Tradition and have served the Catholic Church in a leadership capacity my entire adult life in parishes, universities, dioceses, and national ministry organizations, guiding Church leaders throughout the United States and across the world. My focus has been in pastoral ministry with young Catholics, leadership formation, and consulting with ministry organizations in strategic planning and mission assessment. Throughout, I have continued to volunteer in my parish youth ministry, sacramental preparation activities, and adult faith formation.

I continue to learn from all my sacramental encounters: zealous churchgoers, "nones" who have no religious affiliation, "dones" who used to participate "religiously" and now do not, and "free-range

Catholics" who hold onto their Catholic roots, even as they struggle to find a spiritual home in parishes and Church structures and continue to commit themselves to "what the Church believes." We are all on a shared journey, as we try to find words to express our experiences.

How to Use This Book

This book explores what forms and informs a disciple's heart. I have used the image of "heart" as a prism through which to view a variety of spiritual adventures and how we participate in building the reign of God. Sometimes our activities, ministry, and Church involvement can wear on our spirits, and we don't notice the toll it takes each day or year after year. We keep going, even as the fire that burned in us becomes faint, long after fatigue and disappointment have set in, and even after we have lost heart. This book is intended as a companion to discover the grace that keeps us moving forward in ministry and faith and to reflect on the joy and sorrow, hope and despair that may have overtaken our weary hearts.

At times, we all need to nourish or rejuvenate our spirit and have a "heart-to-heart" with God and ourselves. This book is a first-aid kit of sorts for anyone on a spiritual journey, whether you serve in Church leadership in a formal capacity, participate in faith-sharing settings, or find yourself as a solitary traveler looking for spiritual respite. It is a book to read on your own or with a group; over a series of weeks, the course of a year or more—or whatever works best for you. You can write on these pages or dedicate a writing book or journal to hold your experiences and answer reflection questions. You can make an audio recording of your thoughts if you already spend too much time writing, or just think as you go. I encourage you to read slowly, thoughtfully, and deeply. This book is for you however it might offer refreshment for your heart and spirit.

The Heart of a Disciple includes wisdom I have discovered in my own spiritual journey and is divided up in ways I hope will foster a reflective experience and serve as a guide for an individual or groups. Each chapter begins with a reflective overview of the chapter topic, followed by "A Disciple's Life" to consider a particular experience of our spiritual journey, along with any gained insight or blessing. This section offers an opportunity to remember a moment in life, Church, ministry, or spirituality in a *Cor Divina* (Divine Heart) style of reflection, reminiscent of a *Lectio Divina* (Divine Lesson) pattern of contemplation, but one that focuses on the heart to ask four consistent questions:

- What happened?
- How did you listen to your heart?
- What did you learn?
- What grace was present?

"A Disciple's Heart" then looks at our spiritual journey from the inside out and includes three reflection questions to discuss, write about, share with others, or ponder over time. Each chapter concludes with "Going Forth," to offer suggestions for a spiritual practice or behavior we might incorporate into our lives, followed by a prayer to pray on your own or with others.

No matter where we find ourselves in life, the mission of discipleship remains before us, as does our call to support others on their journey of discovery. Like the Word of God, I hope this collection of ideas, stories, and experiences will light your path, give insight to your heart, and encourage you to explore what fuels you as a pilgrim of faith and strengthens you as a disciple of Jesus Christ. May the Lord bless you and all of us on this journey of past, present, and future discipleship. Amen. +

Chapter 1

A Disciple's Heart

Look for the next handhold.

Discipleship is our *yes* to Jesus. Our yes can flow from a profound encounter with Jesus, a gradual awakening to the deeper life realities Jesus embodied, or a deep hunger yet to be satisfied. As Catholic Christians, our individual yes is strengthened, supported, and nurtured by our yes to the community of believers we are initiated into at our baptism. Our baptism is the source of ministry and the beginning of our call to discipleship. Initiation into our Church challenges us to be active participants, rather than spectators alongside our community of believers.

While we may be formed as Catholics in parishes, faith communities, and multiple catechetical experiences, we are called to live our baptism in all the areas of our lives. This is what I like to call, "discipleship in the marketplace." The "marketplace" is wherever we are, inside or outside a church building—with our families, in our relationships, where we work, and where we play. Our baptismal call to discipleship shapes how we parent, how we work as employees, and how we employ others. Discipleship informs how we live as neighbors and how we engage with our local communities. We can also be called to enact our baptismal call in particular areas of ministry: liturgy, catechesis, faith sharing groups, outreach, hospitality, leadership, or other areas of service. Our service might evolve into a profession or vocation, but it all begins with our baptism and never replaces our discipleship in the marketplace.

The Ministry Road

There are many ways we find our way into ministry. Maybe you grew up in a family where community volunteering became part of your DNA. You were always asked to help out and one thing led to another. Maybe you were invited to a faith sharing or Scripture group, asked to join the choir, or teach in a faith formation program. Perhaps you experienced a conversion that brought you into the Church and ultimately to the work you are doing now. Or you realized you felt a call, went off to school for a degree, and here you are. No matter how we currently share our faith, it is important to remember our baptismal call is always evolving within the Church. Even if we are not sure of our current commitment or participation, we are always on the road together as the reign of God unfolds within and around us.

The Second Vatican Council began on October 11, 1962, and concluded December 8, 1965, as Pope St. John XXIII and then Pope St. Paul VI sought to complete what had begun at the First Vatican Council gathering, held from December 1869 to October 1870. The aim had been to extend ecumenical outreach and address the new needs of the modern world. Those attending Vatican I were estimated at a little more than 2,500, but like Christ's first disciples, their decisions changed the world as the Church considered leadership structures, titles, and how laypeople, religious, and deacons were to share in existing hierarchical and sacramental structures.

Vatican II solidified the discussions begun at Vatican I and brought forth change that continues to inform how Catholics serve as disciples and actively participate in the liturgy as more than onlookers at Mass. Although Catholic laity now attain degrees in many areas of Church ministry, that was not always the case. When the Second Vatican Council called on Catholics to "help Father," many parishioners had no expertise beyond a desire to serve or an inability to say no. Pastors were caught in multiple double binds as they guided others, while still figuring out what to do next. They learned English Mass prayers but weren't sure how to inspire congregations without the clout of "Catholic guilt." And what were they inspiring everyone to do anyway?

The Heart Finds a Way

Next to grandparenting, my favorite hobby is technical rock climbing on the face of a mountain. While the goal to go up or down is pretty straightforward, it is not unusual to get stuck in the middle. We might not see the next step, become paralyzed by elevation, or just get tired of the climb. That's when I find two axioms can be helpful: "look for the next handhold" and "six inches makes all the difference."

While on a rock face, a climber looks for handholds and footholds to support the gradual climb to the summit of the mountain. The handholds can often seem hidden, not easily recognized, and beyond reach, or even nonexistent. However, experienced climbers know that gaining even a few inches in elevation can provide an entirely new perspective. Stepping up brings an unseen view into focus, potential handholds and footholds appear to the climber's sight, and more importantly, a way forward up the mountain.

Church ministry can sometimes feel like we are climbing a rock wall. The work can overwhelm or exhaust us to where we forget our call, feel alone in our ministry, or lose sight of our destination altogether, but we may not be as lost as we think. A change in perspective, unexpected assistance, small accomplishments, or even taking time off can provide us new handholds. One new idea can lead to another and eventually to a solution that can propel us to a whole new view. A disciple's heart understands ministry, not as hours or tasks, but by the presence of Christ we bring through our service.

A disciple's heart holds the fervor of the apostles who cheered Jesus on his way into Jerusalem and stood by him at the foot of the cross. A disciple's heart believes death and resurrection is within everything we encounter and that God will bring life, despite all we might endure. It is my hope this book will offer handholds and encouragement to make the climb a little easier and see the path a little more clearly as we all journey to the kingdom of heaven together. Let's go!

A Disciple's Life

At times, we might doubt our place in the Church, struggle for a sense of purpose, and be distracted by unexpected difficulties, but the mission of Jesus remains, as does our call to share our gift of faith. Parishes without priests can seem an insurmountable challenge, but it also gives us the opportunity to look more closely at parish structures, who we are as active disciples and Catholics, and how to be our best self.

Think of a time when you felt stuck in your spiritual journey.

- What happened?
- How did you listen to your heart?
- What did you learn?
- What grace was present?

A Disciple's Heart

Despite the shared excitement of Vatican II, the road to realizing its vision has not always been easy. For every thriving pastor, youth minister, religious educator, or liturgical musician, there are many who feel isolated, exhausted, and defeated. Rather than look for a more fruitful way to serve, we lose perspective, searching for more hours and energy, no matter the distance between current reality and the call that first drew someone to the Church or ministry.

It is hard to know how to encourage anyone to remain in the Church if they are disillusioned, but almost any time is a great time to be Catholic, especially if you like chaos, which can actually be a gift. God formed the whole of creation out of chaos. And despite all that appears to be out of control, or fighting for control, we are still the Church, and this is where grace dwells. That is where our mission always begins—how do we live as Jesus? How do we live as the Body of Christ?

We are to live as persons of faith and shed light on injustice through our service, wherever we are. When we foster faith in a classroom, preside at the Eucharist, find shelter for someone without a home, visit our isolated neighbor next door, speak out against global injustice or inner-city poverty, we are doing the work Jesus handed on to his disciples to hand on to us.

Another aspect of rock climbing parallels our spiritual journey. Climbers have belayers. Belayers hold the belay line, which is the safety rope connected to the climbers. The belayers watch the climbers and listen for what they need—less slack in the rope or more tension. Belayers hold fast to ensure the safety of the climbers. Even if the climbers lose their grip on the mountain entirely, the fall is minimal, because the climbers are "on belay," and the belayers hold tension on the rope to keep the climbers secure. The bond of trust between climbers and belayers is profound.

We all need belayers. The spiritual journey can include moments that overwhelm us to where we feel stuck on our climb and can't seem to find any handholds. Some days might be hard; on other days, we celebrate keeping our footing as we continue to make progress up the mountain. And here we are, over sixty years after the Second Vatican Council, and we are still exploring how to live and pray as a faith community.

We might doubt our place in ministry, and struggles can distract us from our sense of purpose, but nothing changes the mission Jesus gave us and our charge to share our gifts with others. We need people in our lives to hold our safety line and help us reach higher, as our baptismal call unfolds. Our faith community, our friends, or family might hold the rope for us together, when we attempt difficult climbs. We are not meant to climb alone. Ministry is a community sport!

- Who are the belayers in your life? Who makes sure you are safe?
- How does your community hold you on belay?
- Whom do you hold on belay?

Going Forth

Many roads have been traveled, detours encountered, and new roads forged, since Catholic leaders huddled together like disciples in the upper room, trying to understand their new call after the Second Vatican Council. Hearts and faith were ignited in Catholic schools, religious education classes, and youth ministry events under the guidance of priests, religious, and pastoral ministers as everyone sought to discover a new way of "being Catholic." Our main task is to stay on the journey, step up when we need a new perspective, and trust in the Spirit. Six inches can make all the difference.

Recall how you were first invited to participate in the Church. Write down the names of family, friends, supporters, and colleagues who have walked with you on your journey. Pray in gratitude for them.

Concluding Prayer

God of all life,
you hold us securely in your grasp,
and guide us beyond our sight.

Be with us as we seek to
live and serve
with your heart.

Help us say yes to each step
and trust you are on belay.

Amen +

Chapter 2

A Path with Heart

It is only with the heart that one can see rightly.

I love to travel. Everywhere. Whether I am on Everest or in Antarctica, I can choose to be a tourist or a pilgrim. Travel always includes two trails, one of destination—a trip to a particular place as a tourist—and one of inner purpose. When we set off on a spiritual journey, we become a pilgrim—on the ground, in our mind, within our heart, or all three. The difference between a trip and a journey is that one takes us to a place, and the other takes us inside. The purpose of our journey is our excursion within. This is the beginning of how we live as a disciple.

A trip may include planning and a specific itinerary, but a journey offers a larger vision, one that includes passion, steadfastness, and a commitment to continue regardless of road hazards or struggle. A tourist travels for pleasure, but a pilgrim travels with an inner destination. A tourist takes trips. A pilgrim embarks on a journey that can transport us without our ever leaving our home, church, or backyard. As we become immersed in Scripture, mythology, literature, or experiences of nature, our inner journey might take us places we never thought of traveling. A pilgrim's destination holds inward and outward excursions that lead us toward a higher purpose, and ultimately the kingdom of God. As disciples, all our travels lead us toward or away from this heavenly destination, and what we do each day helps or hinders our journey onward. We can walk with purpose or ignore the calling of our heart. The choice is ours.

Our Path

And then there is the path. While a journey can bring up images of highways, beltways, back roads, and jeep trails, paths are more intimate. Paths carry a vision of forests, mountains, streams, and all those tempting unexplored turns we don't see on the main roads. We can take trips, or we can go on a journey within. The journey within requires we follow the path of our heart.

So why is a path with heart important? As the Cheshire Cat said to Alice in *Alice's Adventures in Wonderland*, "if we don't know where we're going, then it doesn't matter which way we go." And why is a destination important? Because without one, we will never get there, no matter how far we travel, or how long. And without heart, we may not notice when we are lost. Our path with heart leads us forward.

Can you even see your path? Or is any potential trail overgrown with dried bushes and overgrown grass? It might be time for a little landscaping or yardwork! But first you have to find your path, or find it again. Without our heart to guide us, we can end up far from where we started, in places we didn't intend to go. If we are tired, overwhelmed, or depressed, our surroundings might change, without our noticing. What is your terrain? Organized or chaotic? Smooth, rocky, or lined with signs pointing in all different directions? Is your path a comfortable place to spend time? Or maybe your road is so beautiful, you just keep fixing it up and don't take time to walk on it.

Following Our Path

Each day, we make decisions to stay on our path or stray. We can notice what brings life or ignore what erodes our spirit. We can care for our pilgrim path, just maintain the road, or keep stumbling around the potholes that stall us in meaningless activity and fatigue. And while function is vital to the path, the important question is, Where does it lead? Where is your path leading you?

Two trails, outward and inward, form our path. Our outward journey is shaped by our lifestyle, career, vocation, relationships, and all we do each day. Our inward journey is who we are, how we define ourselves, what matters most to us, and how we live our faith. Although our outward journey might be more evident to those around us, our inner trek determines how we act. Our inner path is the still point the Psalmist encourages in Psalm 46, inviting us to know God. Can we be still and know that God is God? This might sound simple, but it can be difficult with the clamor of the potential choices and priorities that surround us, threaten to overwhelm us, or drown us within.

These two distinct inward and outward paths merge to bring harmony or discord to our life and become "our path." As such, it is important to understand what brings us life and what helps or hinders our journey with God. What limits our search for meaning and hope? What distracts or obliterates our inner stillness? What knocks us off our road entirely? Our guiding question is: Does our path have heart? If not, how do we find our true heart and help it flourish?

Embracing Change

The good news is we are not alone on our path. Or at least we don't need to be. We have choices about our companions. Who offers support? What expectations, spoken or unspoken, become disheartening? Who helps us thrive amid any stumble? Who do we want to have with us on our journey?

It is difficult to assess our journey, especially if we don't like what we find. It is harder to realize we need to change. Familiarity can be so comforting. We don't want to make darkness our friend, yet sometimes it is in darkness that we see new light. Few of us want to run into the unknown, but we do it every day. We only think we know what is ahead if we believe we are in control. Some days we are more aware of the light ahead, and don't notice what we are leaving behind. At other times, chaos and emptiness can overtake us and force us to look at what really controls us and what has become our God. Choosing a path with heart, achieving a sense of wholeness, and making "heartfelt" decisions can lead to a greater understanding of ourselves and bring us closer to God. Our pathway is our heart.

A Disciple's Life

Sometimes we need to transform our outer path to find our inner peace. We depend on the practicalities of food, clothing, shelter, a paycheck, and the support of others as a foundation. But sometimes a new beginning requires us to risk and let go, to find a new job, renew or let go of a relationship, or discover an insight that will move us to find what God has in store for us.

Think of a time when you had to make a life-changing decision at work or home.

- What happened?
- How did you listen to your heart?
- What did you learn?
- What grace was present?

A Disciple's Heart

Even when the disciples didn't recognize Jesus on the road to Emmaus, the Gospel of Luke 24:13–35 tells us they listened to their hearts on fire and burning within them. Their hearts told them, this is the Lord! After Jesus ascended, once-timid disciples shared their hearts with the whole world, step-by-step, as they followed their path with hearts that Jesus had formed. Centuries later, we can still listen to our heart to discover our path and who God has made us to be.

When we realize what and who is most important, we can understand more clearly what we need to do to make our priorities a reality. Reflection can help us sense what we might overlook when we are busy. Contemplation can help us learn from the decisions we make, the events we experience, the feelings of being lost, and the struggles to find the right path again. And then we have to walk. Some days we are more confident in our steps as we become more aware of where we are going. Other times, chaos and emptiness force us to look at what has become of our lives and our relationship with God. It is hard to change our habits or embrace the unknown, but sometimes it is required within a din of activity.

Jesus promised us a path with heart. He believed a day would come when we would hear God call us by name, rush from our prodigal ways, sense the strength of God's embrace, and be assured we are on the right road. A day when no door would be sealed against us. A day when our knocking would yield welcome, and a path to love and peace would open. That day can be today and every day as we open our lives to the path God intends. We might still struggle amid difficulties, but God's grace will be with us as we stay on our path.

Scripture and history are full of inspirational people whose lives were changed through encounters with Jesus, and yet they often struggled to find their right path. Peter didn't seem to understand what Jesus meant most of the time, yet he became the foundation of the Church. Mary Magdalene was healed of her demons, became a committed follower of Jesus, and was the first to spread the news of Jesus's resurrection. Mother Theresa's path changed completely after she heard God's call to serve the very poor, sick, and dying people in India.

Sometimes our path can become cluttered with paperwork and busyness. Even good things can sidetrack us and obscure our calling until we don't notice we have lost our way and our heart. But we clear the brush, look for signs to guide us, and get back on the road again. Listening to our heart helps us better understand our path and see our lives in a new way. As we grow from the decisions we make, the events we experience, the people we love, and the sense of being lost, we can more readily find the right path again. This is part of the learning curve of a disciple.

- When do you feel most alive?
- What do you fear most about change?
- When have you felt that you were on the right path? What did you notice?

Going Forth

When our choices are based on love and faith, we develop an inner compass that connects us to our true self and God within. Our disciple's heart guides our inner compass to form our outer path. Antoine de Saint-Exupéry's *The Little Prince* tells us, "It is only with the heart that one can see rightly; what is essential is invisible to the eye." This is how we find our path—with our heart.

Sit quietly, palms up, and listen to your heart beat.
Imagine your path with heart. What do you see? Step out.

Concluding Prayer

Ever-present God,
your holy compass
guides us on our path.

Help us to find you,
and hear you in our hearts.

May we always
see and know
rightly with your love.

Amen +

Chapter 3

A Heart for Ministry

Heartsight becomes our path forward.

It can seem somewhat daunting to set off on a new faith journey by ourselves, but on the path, we are never alone in the Body of Christ. We may lose our way and lose our path, but then we get back on the road and strike out once again. Beyond any obstacle, pain, loneliness, or fear, God's forgiveness and guidance always offer us a way back to the right path. It may take time and more than a little effort, but the path is there, waiting for us to listen to our inner voice, to remember our best understanding and love, to hold it in our memory, and to reconnect with purpose once again.

Remembering connects us to the essence of a past event. We re-member, recall, and turn our sights to the future. When we feel lost, we can pause and remember when we last walked with heart. Where we were, who we were, and who we were with on our path. Remembering can move us forward.

Finding Our Path

But how do we find our path? And where do we begin? Back to Alice and her adventure in Wonderland. When the Cheshire Cat asked her where she wanted to go, her reply was, "I don't much care where." That's why the cat wisely told her it didn't matter which way she went. Destination is immaterial if our heart is not in it. Heart and desire make all the difference. If we don't care what we are doing or where we are going, then it doesn't matter what we do. We wander aimlessly. We can work anywhere, for anyone, without doing anything that brings us life. Or we can look to the heart, courage, and faith of those who walked their path before us and find ours.

For many years, my wife, Maggie, and I hosted a week-long wilderness retreat. Each summer, we would gather a group of adventurous souls to rock climb and cave in West Virginia. The days held a lot of physical exertion, but at night we took time to reflect on our experiences around the campfire, and we used climbing and caving as images for the spiritual journey.

One of the more dramatic moments of the week took place in a cave when we turned off our headlamps and were plunged into immediate darkness. Not a sliver of light was present. At first, the impenetrable darkness was overwhelming. But then other senses began to kick in and compensate, straining for some certainty against the blackness. Even silence seemed to magnify as an imagined "hearing" of darkness appeared to take hold. Eventually, every drop of water, clearing of a throat, and flap of an unseen bat became a clue to orient us beyond feeling trapped by the lack of light.

This "increased hearing" is exactly what we need on our path of discipleship. But first, we need to turn off our headlamps to recognize what distracts us, what prevents us from clearly seeing or hearing or following God's call each day. Perceived darkness can become light when we understand what is holding us back from our true calling and limiting our life of discipleship. Then, any point of light can become a potential exit out of our cave and back to our path.

Heartsight

In the same way, listening in a dark cave can improve our hearing, we can also develop "heartsight," a spiritual version of night goggles to light our way. Heartsight is more than eyesight. Heartsight guides our spirit to see with our whole self and whole heart. Heartsight sees beyond the unlovable, impossible, and seemingly insurmountable. We become more aware of the presence and movement of God in our lives and the lives of others. When we "see" with our heart, the Spirit becomes more present. Our focus on our needs and immediate gratification becomes less pressing as our heartsight helps us see what is really important and we respond accordingly—with heart.

Developing heartsight is not for the faint of heart, however. Warnings abound: Don't make emotional decisions! Don't be so passionate! You're not thinking straight! The Tin Man in the *Wizard of Oz* was advised more than once that it was better not to have a heart, unless it was unbreakable. And yet all he wanted was to be human, gentle, sentimental, loving, and friendly, all of which he believed were found in a heart. All of which often seem impractical, superfluous, or unproductive. Still, the Tin Man believed "with all his heart" that a real heart would make him whole.

Sometimes the hardest part of any journey is to give up the known for the unknown and just get started. Even when our inner voice has said go, it can be hard to follow. Bilbo Baggins of *The Hobbit* went on the journey of his lifetime, but he did not go easily, and he found it hard to leave the complacent comfort of his Shire home. Enter Wizard Gandalf who helped Bilbo realize his choice was between isolation in the Shire and the future he feared. But Bilbo needed to freely choose his path. He could not be forced onto the road, or he most likely would have fought heavily to get back to the security he valued more than any possible adventure ahead.

When Bilbo returned to his home in the Shire, he was not the same hobbit who had left a year earlier. He had been changed by his journey. He had loved his adventure but was at peace to be back home. He was at home in himself in the company of his path with heart. He had acquired heartsight.

What stops us from stepping onto a new path in our life or discipleship? Why do we doubt and disregard promptings that tell us our heart just "isn't in it"? Why do we remain in a job, a relationship, a region of the country, a profession, or any situation that fails to bring life, that fails to have heart? What would prompt us to follow our heart?

A Disciple's Life

Heartsight lights our path as we listen to the Spirit and discern our path forward. But it is not without cost. Heartsight is often born of pain, risk, and most of all, love. As we grow in heartsight, we see "more than meets the eye." Not only with our eyes and heart, but with the love of God. And like love, heartsight finds a way through everything—everything.

Think of a time you made a decision about your life, career, vocation, friendship, or other crossroads.

- What happened?
- How did you listen to your heart?
- What did you learn?
- What grace was present?

A Disciple's Heart

Although there are no spelunking stories in Scripture, unless we count Elijah hiding in the cave in 1 Kings 19:20, we can imagine the disciples experiencing the blackness of no hope as Jesus was placed in a cave-like tomb cut out of rock. Or we can see them creating their own cave in the upper room, afraid they would suffer the same fate as Jesus if they were called out as his followers. But what light they must have experienced in the days after the resurrection!

Sometimes, all we want is a cave, but we are to be people of light! What were you doing the last time you were genuinely happy? What brings you back to your best self where you hear God inside you? What inspires you when you are tired, discouraged, or feel lost? Sometimes darkness is the only way we can see any sliver of new light to discover our purpose. At the end of their lives, salmon are drawn back to the very stream of their birth. Once there, they lay their eggs and die in a seeming tragic end, but in reality, it is the expression of their destiny. They come back to their beginnings to give life again. We begin our lives as Catholics marked with the sign of the cross blazed across our foreheads. This marking connects us with all disciples—past, present, future, and around the globe. This is the beginning of "our path."

Joseph probably thought his life's work was to be a carpenter, and yet his occupation is only a footnote in the greater story of salvation. Had he not listened to the angel in his dream, life would have been much different for all of us. The first disciples left all they knew to follow Jesus into unexpected events and miracles. They were fisherman, tax collectors, lepers, merchants, outcasts, multiple "Marys," and nameless thousands, who gathered on hillsides and ate food that seemed to appear from nowhere. They listened to a message that changed their lives and ultimately the whole world. Their courage and commitment led them to the cross, the resurrection, and to the ends of the earth to give witness to all they had absorbed as a follower of Jesus.

It is important to learn to recognize our path. When we pay attention to what brings us joy and what we love best, we may more easily see where our path is leading. If we can consecrate these moments in our memory, they can become like a baptismal garment to gather around us and infuse us, when we most need to remember who we are each day. Then we can look back at the grace that has formed our heart and look forward to where we feel called to step next on our path.

We share the same path and purpose as those disciples who followed Jesus, but we have one great advantage—we know the rest of the story. Life comes from death! And we know the game plan: Live as Jesus did, seek our path, use our gifts to serve the world. Listen, learn, act, repeat. Jesus's first disciples must have wondered, more than once, if they were crazy or doing the right thing, but they followed their heartsight and blazed a trail for all future faithful to follow. So can we.

- Where do you most often see light in your life?
- What is your greatest gift? How do you use it?
- When do you hear God most clearly?

Going Forth

The journey changes us. We may feel secure and confident at times and think we know where we are going. Then we get lost, or there is unexpected road construction. But if we follow our heart, the life, death, and resurrection of Jesus will lead us to our path and on our journey home. We have only to seek God, listen to our heart, and make the best choice. Then we keep walking.

Write down a favorite memory from childhood, then one from each decade of your life and today.

What is similar? What has changed? Put a star beside what brought you the most life.

Concluding Prayer

Eternal God,
you give us
a purpose and path
to share your love.

Help us to
see with your heart
in the dark and
in the light.

May we listen
to your voice within.
Each day.

Amen +

Chapter 4

A Transcendent Heart

The challenge is to see God now.

Iconic fairy-tale writer Hans Christian Andersen tells us, "The whole world is a series of miracles, but we're so used to them we call them ordinary things." As Catholics, we live in a sacramental world, where everything is more than it seems. All of creation reflects its Creator and is filled with a divine presence that transcends all that surrounds us. But in order to live a transcendent life, we need to look with the eyes of our heart. Mystics and mystagogues used their heartsight or "sight inside" into the mysteries of life to help others understand God more fully. For example, after new Christians were baptized, teachers of the mysteries, known as mystagogues, helped them unfold the sacramental mysteries they had just experienced and put words to that experience. While mystagogues were teachers, mystics were those who gave themselves over to the divine in order to grow in their relationship and understanding of God. Mystics sought to transcend the bounds of earthly knowledge to encounter the Creator within themselves and to engage the world with the eyes of the soul.

The Eyes of the Soul

We might look back to a particular time in our life and be able to see how one event led to another. During times of struggle, our life might not make sense, but in retrospect, we might see God was present more clearly than we thought. The challenge is to see God now, rather than in our rearview mirror. We might see God's hand more easily when we experience goodness, beauty, or love, but what about in our pain or woundedness? This is when it can be vital to see with the eyes of our soul, to see God now.

In his book, *The Soul's Journey into God*, theologian and philosopher St. Bonaventure refers to opening the "eyes of our souls" in order to find God's peace. But first, he cautions, we must know who we are within Creation in order to enter into our soul. The eyes of the soul don't necessarily change what is before us, but we are able to see differently. Our heartsight awakens us to the presence of God around us and the light of God within us. Heartsight helps us see the Spirit and notice more readily when it is not present. The Spirit magnifies everything to help clarify what might otherwise seem intangible or beyond our grasp.

While the Spirit is intangible, it demands expression, and gives us meaning and direction. So much so, we are drawn by it and to it. Parishes can have beautiful church buildings, a large formal staff, and seemingly all the right programs, but without the Spirit, there will be little engagement, connectedness, or shared purpose. When we see the world with a transcendent heart, we look for the presence of God in almost everything and everyone. In the light of the kingdom, we see the world differently; we see with the eyes of our soul. The world becomes transcendent, and every situation, personal interaction, or outcome takes on a new meaning.

Transcendent Sight

Some people seem naturally filled with an enthusiasm for life, full of joy, and in touch with their soul. They see the world through the lens of the Spirit and God's activity. Others seem empty, perhaps filled with a sadness that permeates their lives. Even if good things are present, they seem not to notice genuine beauty, joy, love, or the richness of life amid their despondency and, perhaps, lack an appreciation for music, art, dance, sculpture, literature, or children. Yet joy can be contagious. We could all use a little practice finding joy and seeing the Spirit, just like practicing any sport or musical instrument. Even St. Mother Teresa learned to see God anew. She was content to work as a teacher on behalf of the poor until she received what she called "a second calling" on a train on the way to a retreat.

Before that life-changing train ride, she knew "of" the poor, but did not feel compelled to change her life with the Sisters of Loreto. She "looked" at the poor around her but did not really "see" them, until that train ride. That's when she really saw them and began to experience poverty firsthand, out in the streets, where she cared for those who were outcasts, marginalized by poverty and disease. She wanted everyone to know of God's overwhelming love, no matter their life situation. She eventually established a missionary arm of the Sisters of Loreto that lived up to its name, *Missionaries of Charity*. She built open-air schools and a home for the dying, and she helped those living in poverty all over the world. Mother Teresa did what all disciples are to do. She saw, listened, spread the word about what God can do, and helped others do the same.

Sometimes we have to let go of one image to see another more clearly. Or concentrate in a different way. But the more we do it, the better we become at seeing. Like the black and white of negative and positive space. An image in the white area is more evident, then you look again to see something entirely new as the black area forms a new shape. This is why we need a transcendent heart—a heart that sees beyond the noise and the swirl of our day, a heart with high beams to cut through any fog or darkness. It is not easy to see more than meets the eye, but it is a far greater loss to miss the sacred miracles before us.

A Disciple's Life

It might be hard to notice something we haven't thought was important. We might feel like we're just not going to gain heart-sight. But gradually, like looking at one of those paintings that seem like just specks of color until an image emerges, we can begin to see the picture. But first we have to "see."

Think of a time you were unable to see God's presence.

- What happened?
- How did you listen to your heart?
- What did you learn?
- What grace was present?

A Disciple's Heart

We can imagine mystagogues, mystics, and saints seeing the world with spiritual eyes, perhaps effortlessly, but what about us? What if we have no experience with spirituality? What if we are not a natural at seeing with our soul? Or even going with our gut? As in any new venture, we can learn. We can train ourselves to see the transcendent—to see differently. It just takes a little practice.

First, we need to pause. In a complex and chaotic world, stopping can become a spiritual skill. We might need to practice pausing as we're racing through a busy day, a rushed morning, a festive evening, or a week of duties that never seem to end. By pausing, we might begin to see what is happening around us. What is really happening, right in front of us. What do you see? Who do you talk with, and what do you hear? Are you really listening? Are you really present? And where is the Holy Spirit in any given moment? A transcendent heart, along with our heartsight, helps us be present in the moment and look with the eyes of our soul and spirit, and all the other senses God gave us with which to serve and love. What do you see when you really look inside and around you? Do you see the world full of miracles?

Seeing with spiritual eyes lets us appreciate what we love and notice what we are doing right. These insights and understandings give us strength when we meet trials. That is why we must first learn to see with our soul. A transcendent heart alerts us to when we have lost sight and brings us back to our path.

I have developed two practices to deepen my ability to "see" God's presence. The first happens as people receive communion at Mass in my parish. I watch people in line as they move toward the altar and when they come back down the aisle to their pews. I only know them as mutual parishioners, but I recognize that they each hold multifaceted life experiences—joys and sufferings, love and loss, achievements and disappointments. And yet, we walk the same line, and share in the same Eucharist each week, around a table where all are one in our one Lord. This is a profound experience.

Second, when I'm in an airport or store, out walking, enjoying nature, at work, in family gatherings, or wherever I find myself, I have started to ask, "Where do I see the kingdom of God breaking through?" I look for God's presence. It's easy to see when surrounded by peace, love, or joy, but what about when things are not going as well? We also need to see God's presence in brokenness, pain, and suffering. As disciples of Jesus, we must name the evil within violence, racism, oppression, poverty, and all who seek to do harm, but it is essential to see the resurrection, despite the crucifixion. We need to remind ourselves that God does not abandon anyone during hard times. Seeing beyond struggle is not always easy, but that is why we practice. That is how we gain a transcendent heart.

- When is it hardest for you to see the presence of God?
- Who do you consider a mystic in your life?
- When do you most experience God's presence?

Going Forth

Have you ever noticed how intently people watch slide shows or look at photo displays? Vacations, family gatherings, and important life events are all suspended from time, just for a moment. Everything happens far too quickly in real time. We may not notice all the details until we pause and still our minds and hearts—just for a moment—until our spirit catches up with the grace right in front of us.

Gather images for a slide show or photo display that express God's presence for you. What themes emerge?

Concluding Prayer

Transcendent God,
your miracles are all around
and in us.

Help us to pause
and see you
EVERYWHERE.

Open our eyes
to your mysteries
and our hearts
to your view.

Amen +

Chapter 5

The Dream of the Heart

Death: Been there. Done that. No fear!

There is nothing like a detour or a road construction sign to put a damper on any journey. Even a few feet of delay can feel like an eternity. At times, our journey of discipleship might feel the same. We become fatigued, struggle, and doubt if we're doing the right thing. Some days might feel like a tennis match as our emotions are volleyed back and forth, and the best we can do is to hope for some balance. But then there are moments of pure joy, restoration, laughter, and peace.

I often find the source of any restlessness to be when I am caught between two contrasting dreams: the societal dream and the Jesus dream. These dreams become fundamental in how we understand our lives and create meaning to inform our lifestyle, relationships, and goals. The Jesus dream offers everlasting life. But the societal dream has better marketing, fueled by bottomless advertising, more money, television, and various forms of social media.

The societal dream calls us to be beautiful, athletic, entertaining, successful, and above all, rich. The societal dream endorses materialism, competition, individualism, self-indulgence, and a quicksand consumerism that pulls us further into the illusion that we "need" whatever the dream offers. The societal dream perceives a world of scarcity, where there is not enough "good stuff" to go around or meet everyone's needs. The societal dream runs on a perpetual loop in the background of our lives. Though unattainable by most, we can unknowingly absorb its urgent imperative to compete for natural resources, material goods, and money. Eventually we might think we also need to fight for respect, power, glory, recognition, and perhaps even love.

When we are afraid that we don't have enough, everyone around us becomes competition, a replaceable means to an end, or an obstacle on our way to "the top." New people, cultures, and ideas become potential threats to the status quo, existing power, and unchallenged domination. We build walls to protect what we think others might want, rather than welcoming mutual support. A scarcity mentality erodes our generosity, affects our worldview, and infects our dream, like a virus spreading throughout our life. We begin to think that if someone gets a bigger piece of the pie, we will get less. We don't trust God's abundance and barely trust our own.

Living the Dream

Thank goodness we have the Jesus dream. This dream holds the fullness of abundant life Jesus offers us in the Gospel of John 10:10. This is a dream that draws us toward people and community, compassion, mercy, love, joy, and liberation. The Jesus dream calls us to look at inner dignity, where everyone has something to offer and contribute. There is room at the table for everyone, not just limited seating for celebrities or those who hold financial access.

In Luke 4:1–13, following his baptism by John in the Jordan River, Jesus withdraws for forty days to the desert. I have always thought of this sojourn as preparation for his mission. We all have our desert experiences where life's difficulties can tempt us to abandon our journey, but they can also make us stronger. Jesus withstood all glimmers of possessions and power, temptations of celebrity, glory, success, and invincibility, because he knew who he was and more importantly "whose" he was.

After Jesus returns from the desert, Luke 4:14–15 tells us that news of him has spread throughout the region where he taught in synagogues and received acclaim. He eventually returns to his hometown of Nazareth and goes to the synagogue. Jesus stands up to read and opens the scroll to the prophet Isaiah. But this isn't just any passage; Isaiah 61 is an exceptional passage that identifies the speaker as the Messiah. Jesus embodies the Scripture as he announces he is the anointed one, sent by the Spirit of the Lord to bring liberty and healing to the poor, the captive, and the oppressed. In the proclamation, Jesus presents a vision of how life on earth should imitate the reign of God. This event marked the beginning of his public ministry, but also the beginning of his road to crucifixion—how could a local from Nazareth claim to be the Messiah?

Later in his ministry, Jesus would continue to turn culture and expectation on its head. Mathew 25:31–46 tells us how he proclaims care for the least as an entrance requirement to heaven, rather than authority or prestige. The vision Jesus proclaimed in Nazareth remains for disciples today. The poor, the captive, the blind, and the oppressed are still with us throughout the world, wracked by poverty, persecution, and war. Closer to home, leaders and community organizers grapple with the effects of racism, gun violence, deprivation, and discrimination.

The Jesus dream is urgent, calling us to heal and binding us with all those in need, not only the economically poor, but those who are emotionally poor, captive to unhealthy pursuits, toxic relationships, and addiction. We may not be physically blind, but we can be blind to the injustices that enslave and oppress those struggling around us, those who bear the weight of expectations and are vulnerable to the dangers of a life without hope. Jesus proclaims freedom and jubilee to everyone. We are the disciples who help make this reality possible as we remember the Jesus dream, share it, believe it, and live it. Each day. Dreams really can come true!

A Disciple's Life

Our dreams are the first indicators of our path. But sometimes we get sidetracked by a quest for security. It is easy to go no further than the idea. We fear losing possessions or relationships, making a bad decision or impression, or standing out for standing up for the "wrong" person or value. The reality is we do not need to be stuck in scarcity. We can choose a new path and start a new dream, one that gives life, rather than draws it from us. The Jesus dream tells us there is enough Spirit for everyone.

Recall a time when you were caught between societal dreams and the Jesus dream.

- What happened?
- How did you listen to your heart?
- What did you learn?
- What grace was present?

A Disciple's Heart

It is not always easy to answer the call of discipleship amid crowds of seemingly successful societal dreamers. But the resurrection empowers us to pull on our Jesus T-shirt that declares, "Death: Been there. Done that. No fear!" The Jesus dream immerses us in a forever kind of abundance. Jesus modeled what it means to live and love completely, and he brings his message to those who are alone, in need, or marginalized. Sometimes the societal dream looks attractive when we feel stranded in the dry, barren, loneliness of a desert that seems unbearable. But the oasis is a mirage, the societal dream is not real and holds no love, completeness, or integrity. The societal dream tells us to live fast but not deep. Relationships might be plentiful but not committed. And gospel values can be replaced by a consumerism Christianity that can appear cultic more than inclusive and promote a cushy and militant individualism.

Living well and enjoying personal pursuits are not sinful in and of themselves, but when they become a substitute for God or benchmarks to beat down and compete against others, we fall victim to a scarcity mentality. Politics, sports, financial wealth, social status, possessions, and gourmet food and drink can potentially bring us together, but they can also evolve into rival paths that can influence how we relate to one another. When any of these "good things" become more important than the care of the person next to us, they become a false idol that defines what and who is valuable. And whoever has the most wins.

Ironically, the word *compete* derives from the Latin, *competere*, meaning to "strive in common." If we are busy being *with* one another, we spend less time striving against one another. There is room for only one champion in the societal dream, but everyone has a place in the Body of Christ. Everyone is enough.

If we do not live the dream God has given us, we are like a pilgrim who stands on the side of the road, hesitant to step out on the journey. We can be trapped by our fear. Many people have known fear, violence, abuse, and addiction. They need the liberating news that the darkness doesn't win. At some point in our life journey, we will most likely experience pain, death, loneliness, brokenness, and woundedness. We might only see a shard of light and will need to know and believe it leads to resurrection. While societal and corporate dreams drive us to succeed, Jesus responds to our real and at times desperate hunger for healing, meaning, belonging, justice, and holiness.

As disciples, we are called to help others face fear, violence, abuse, disillusionment, addiction, and failure. We don't have to compete with the societal dream, or a societal Christianity. Jesus provides us an abundance of dignity and value beyond possessions, capacity, fashion sense, or net worth. Everyone has something to contribute within the abundance of the kingdom. Whatever we doubt, whatever we question, life always wins. God wins. Resurrection always overcomes death. This is the Jesus Dream.

- What is your dream?
- What keeps you from acting on your dream?
- How can Jesus help you fulfill your dream?

Going Forth

Jesus calls everyone to his dream of the kingdom of God. We need to believe his dream in order to embrace it and make it real for all who desperately need to be free of poverty, violence, tyranny, abuse, slavery, and suppression. Get real. Stay on your path. Follow your Jesus dream. This is how we build the reign of God. The Jesus dream offers challenges but also transformation.

Plan how you can make the Jesus dream real to someone. Do it. Now plan out another way. And another, and another…

Concluding Prayer

Abundant God,
your dream offers
a seat at the table
for everyone.

All are welcome,
all are worthy,
all are sacred.

Today we say no
to societal dreams
and yes to you.

Amen +

Chapter 6

A Catholic Heart

The cross is where every journey begins.

A "Catholic" heart sees differently. Our baptism and Catholic beliefs provide a lens through which we relate to the universe and all creation in a particular way. Our encounters with God and our spiritual journey hold a particular meaning that includes more than just ourselves. While novels, movies, and television shows often emphasize Catholic symbols as somewhat magical, where statues and images are idolized, or rituals appear to be incantations, a deeper religious awareness is anchored in a Catholic heart.

Catholics experience God in many ways. "Both/and" is a way of life. Jesus lived as true God and true man. We are a people of contemplation and active service. We gather for communal public ritual, but we are fueled by private prayer and devotion. The Catholic Church has built great cathedrals and vital soup kitchens. We are a community of cloistered nuns, a field hospital of missionaries, and a family of parishes around the globe. Echoes of Catholic chant are heard in abbeys throughout the world, alongside animated music at youth gatherings, traditional hymns, gospel spirituals, and songs of praise from every genre. The Eucharist is both bread and flesh, wine and blood. We are potentially saints but also sinners. The contradictions go on and on.

In essence, Catholicism beckons us to view all life in a way that reflects God's presence. We are a sacramental people with a sacramental language that expands the breadth of how Catholics understand God in the world and in heaven. Catholics remember anamnestically as we recall the reality of what happened in the past, remember it in the present, and look forward to its fullness in the future. This remembering is the central mystery of our faith: Christ has died, Christ is risen, Christ will come again. It is the paschal mystery of Jesus passing from death to life and living forever. It is our promise that we will too.

Symbols of the Road

The act of Jesus dying on the cross is where every journey begins, and it is our pathway to heaven. On Holy Thursday, we usher in three days of remembering Christ's death and resurrection from Good Friday to Easter Sunday. We begin by celebrating our call to holiness with the two acts Jesus shared with his disciples before he died: breaking bread and washing feet. Holy Thursday reminds us to do the same every day as a people of community, justice, and the Eucharist. Together, we are the Body of Christ with a shared call to live like Jesus, serve the common good, and build the reign of God.

Every Good Friday, we raise the cross high and remind ourselves we can touch death yet still find the hope of Easter, even in the worst circumstances. Catholics hold multiple contradictions of meaning as we embrace a reality of the cross that is not always as beautiful as in the ceremonies where we remember its power. Spiritual deserts are also a contradiction. Their solitude allows us to face our real self with no distraction, but being left to ourselves might cause us to flee inside. We might not know we are in a desert and be driven to act in ways that separate us further from God and others. Deserts can become pivotal to finding our path, even as we despair at being lost and wandering.

Suffering is similar, in that it brings pain but can also help us feel more deeply, see more clearly, and understand others with more empathy. Suffering can strengthen our resolve to live as our true selves. As Catholics, we live with both feet on the ground, but with our eyes looking to the kingdom. We live on earth and in heaven, between what is and what is unfolding, where we are and where we're going, who we are and who we are called to be. The holy lens of Catholicism impacts where we encounter God, how we relate to the universe and all creation, and how we understand our spiritual journey. All these paradoxes of symbol, reality, humanness, holiness, and heaven are held in the heart of a Catholic disciple. Or they can be, as we grow and continue our path.

Sacraments

Symbols point to a heavenly reality and simultaneously remind us of our path and purpose. That is why symbols and sacraments are so important. Water is not just water, but our baptismal initiation to becoming citizens of heaven. Bread is not only bread, but what gathers us around the eucharistic table. On Holy Saturday, fire is not just fire, but the light and resurrection of Christ. When we stand in a communion line, it might seem like standing in line at a bank or grocery store, but it is not. Each time we walk to receive the body and blood of Jesus, we rehearse our pilgrim path to the heavenly banquet.

Sacraments use symbols to act out heavenly realities on earth. Our actions have that same power. When we welcome others to church, we imitate God welcoming them into the kingdom. All we do inside the church rehearses what we are to do outside. During the liturgy we hear the story of Jesus, and like eucharistic bread, we are blessed, broken, and sent into the world so that people no longer see us but Jesus. Our decision to act as Jesus can change lives as it spills into everything we do. Our care and love can transform others. This is how we become sacramental people.

Each week, the Church gathers to share stories handed down from prophets, apostles, and our ancestors in faith. They are our trailblazers, yet even they did not always seem to understand what God had in store—that death does not win. Jesus lives on through the resurrection and in his disciples today. We are blessed to have so many examples of faithful followers who, like us, were trying their best to follow the road Jesus laid out for them. We are one with their legacy and purpose and continue the road they have paved here and on their way to heaven.

A Disciple's Life

We all experience doubt and confusion. Perhaps we have questioned decisions and choices we have made, we're unsure about our lifestyle or occupation, or we feel uncertain about the direction we are heading. Heart attacks or sudden tragedies give rise to questions of life's meaning, purpose, and worth. But we are not alone. We are family through the cross, bound together, with the heart of a disciple beating inside.

Think of a time when the Church helped you find your way or a sense of purpose.

- What happened?
- How did you listen to your heart?
- What did you learn?
- What grace was present?

A Disciple's Heart

It is not uncommon to come across markings while hiking. Shapes attached to mountains, arrows painted in caves, piled cairns of stones, ribbons, colorful blazes on trees, and images of all kinds have guided hikers, rock climbers, spelunkers, and those who walked the earliest of ancient pilgrimage routes. These markings show us we're on the right track. The first explorers blazed the way so others could more easily follow their trail, hence the term *trailblazer*. Paying attention to our inner markings on our path with heart can be just as valuable. The Church uses signposts as well, where everything from peacocks to pelicans, scallop shells and seashells, copper pots, basins, lilies, and towels all tell the story of our faith.

Catholic sacraments, signs, and symbols connect us to God and to one another as they guide us on our earthly pilgrimage and communicate God's presence to us through the stories of our faith—past, present, and future. They offer us a view of a world of wonder, grace, and miracles, with the beauty of God right in front of us or just below the surface. At times it might be hard to see, but if we stay on our path and look with our heartsight, we become more practiced at noticing the fullness and presence of God all around us. St. Irenaeus summed up this reality in the late second century saying, "The glory of God is the human person fully alive." Like the first disciples, our lives can tell the story of the resurrection and lead others to liberation. This is the holiness to which we are all called, in our hearts, on our paths, and as we work to build the kingdom of God.

The cross is one of the Church's primary symbols, with an intersection that points us vertically to God and horizontally to our journey with others. We share our commitment in the cross with believers across the world and with centuries of disciples who have come before us on unlikely routes. For example, the Apostle Paul was bent on killing Christians until he encountered the power of God on the road to Damascus. Although Jesus struggled in the Garden of Gethsemane, he believed God's love would prevail against the betrayal and the suffering that lay ahead. Jesus thought he was abandoned, yet that evening became the entrance of his path to resurrection.

The cross reminds us, over and over again, of the courage that fuels the hearts of all disciples. Jesus calls us to surrender to love, share all that we have, and fear nothing because God gives us everything. Many holy heroes have experienced spiritual crisis—spiritual heart attacks—but lived to make a difference. So much so that we know their names: Aloysius Gonzaga, Dorothy Day, Augustine, Josephine Bakhita, Oscar Romero, and countless others.

Jesus loved those who were poor and marginalized and exemplified how we can do the same. While the structures of the Catholic Church can seem complicated and antiquated at times, we share the same goals: to follow the example of Jesus, keep Jesus alive through the Word of God, and share in the compassion of God by serving as disciples.

- What Catholic symbol guides you most each day?
- When do you struggle most as a disciple?
- How has the desert formed your spiritual life?

Going Forth

Jesus is the heart of Catholicism, and he created a community of believers that changed the world. His life is our model to let go of superficial facades and entrust ourselves to the compassionate and accepting love of God. Let us embrace, celebrate, and share all we have been given and make the sacred visible to those around us.

Sit in a Catholic church by yourself and look at the images and symbols surrounding you.

Think about how Catholic rituals, practices, and symbols have formed your faith.

Concluding Prayer

Universal God,
your love lives within us
and in all we see—
past, present, and future.

Pain and struggle
are not an end,
but signs of life
yet to come.

In you, we are fully alive,
beyond any death.

Amen +

Chapter 7

A Faithful Heart

Hope has two lovely daughters: anger and courage.

A friend once told me, "The Church is an acquired taste." Church participation can drain us and challenge our passion, but somehow, we keep going. It is hard to be faithful during disheartening situations: clergy misconduct and abuse, theological and clerical tension, ambivalent friends or colleagues, financial tumult, and the general highs and lows of "as the Church turns." The effects of public scrutiny and Church disgrace make our prayer for transformation all the more necessary, but our instincts might urge us to step back in frustration or leave the Church entirely. Our hearts might tell us it is worth the struggle and sacrifice to stay true to our path as part of the Church, but our heads might beg to differ. We keep perspective by listening to our hearts, especially when we encounter difficult terrain.

The Church is not an end in itself but a means to an end—to build the kingdom of God, together. As earthbound Christians, we live within the limits of the real and the ideal as we share a path where history, nostalgia, and rebellion all coexist in the present day within one Church. Can we live with that? More importantly, how do we live with that? What do we share beyond seeming incongruency? We are disciples who try to serve and be like Jesus. In many different ways, but together, we are the Church. We might never get it right, but being perfect is not our goal. We are the ultimate "Practicing Catholics."

At times, we fail, but Scripture and history are full of committed failing followers of faith, who struggled to find their right path, make right decisions, and understand what God wants them to do. And it took them a while! I think of saints as sinners who didn't quit. They found ways to maintain their faithfulness. So can we. You might already be doing it, whether you are in the Church for the long haul, taking a break, or just taking time to decide. It is important to know what you need on your journey and what you already possess.

Perhaps you are more hopeful than you realize, or you draw strength from unidentified sources. Those on the journey with our struggling Church find ways to maintain faithfulness, even if it means stepping back for a moment or discovering sustenance through trial and error. To remain faithful, you can listen to your heart, discern your path, identify what supports or erodes your faith. Then ask yourself, what would make a difference today?

Although it's not always easy to be Catholic, today can be an exciting time to serve the Church, even if the path is not straight. Parishes without full-time priests can give birth to a new vision for lay ministry and provide a broader foundation for parish leadership. Societal injustice can lead Catholics to participate in political arenas and harness the insight and power of pastoral letters to promote the common good. During the COVID-19 pandemic, the Church livestreamed Mass and provided faith formation opportunities for all ages. The pandemic raised awareness for how to connect more with homebound parishioners and support anyone who felt isolated.

Who would have expected new ministries to emerge during such a difficult time? Yet God's grace can show us how to live as problem-solving disciples who bring life—even during a worldwide pandemic. Who knows what goodness might lie ahead if we remain faithful to our path? The journey is not just one day, but every day. Today might be a struggle, but tomorrow could bring more fruit than we might have imagined!

Maintaining Faithfulness

Even when we are doing exactly what we believe to be God's plan, we might feel called to do something new, become disillusioned, or tire of hard days. The path is not always obvious or easy. We might unknowingly spend time on deceptive trails to nowhere, fall down rabbit holes, lose sight of our goals, or abandon our mission altogether as we try to survive each day. Sometimes Church herself creates the barriers and frustrations. This is when we most need support, but by then, we might reject it. Sometimes we wonder if we are enough, if we have the integrity, courage, and capacity demanded by discipleship. This is when we need "heart" to follow our heart.

St. Augustine tells us that, "Hope has two lovely daughters: anger and courage." Anger reminds us things are not the way they should be, and courage is how we make things right. Together, anger and courage can sustain a faithful heart, move us to action, and guard against discouragement—if we can see past our disappointment, resentment, sadness, and a myriad of valid, yet distracting, emotions. However, if we pretend we are untouched by scandalous or life-draining situations in the Church, we can fall into a defensive retreat where denial can keep our heart safe but also numb us into apathy, isolation, or bitterness.

Embracing rough trails is hard, but it also offers the upright courage and hope we need to stay committed to the mission that first stirred our hearts. We may be tempted to think another way is better, but if we know our path and stay on it, we can keep going, despite all circumstances that might discourage us.

Many of my favorite Church heroes—Thomas Aquinas, Pierre Teilhard de Chardin, Karl Rahner, and Archbishop Oscar Romero—all criticized the Church. They were not afraid to declare their displeasure, but they did so as a full member of the body they served. They endured and maintained their faithfulness. Despite exasperated hearts, these disciples continued to help move the Church beyond tragic events, to reform structures, and guide its doctrine. They loved the Church enough to remain faithful and eager for her to grow, no matter her limits, faults, and weaknesses. These legends of faith, along with the whole Communion of Saints, model how we can maintain a faithful heart.

A Disciple's Life

Sometimes we don't notice we have withdrawn from what we used to love the most, but it might be obvious to those around us. That's why it's so important to stay in touch with other pilgrims. We are not meant to maintain faithfulness alone. Even Jesus had a community. Despite struggle, grace can still be present.

Think of a time when you doubted your faith, your commitment to the Church, or discipleship.

- What happened?
- How did you listen to your heart?
- What did you learn?
- What grace was present?

A Disciple's Heart

Faithfulness means to stay the course. But faithfulness also means to come back, if we have left our path, accidentally or intentionally. Difficult stretches of road can prompt us to revisit the communities and companions who first inspired our journey of discipleship. Or we can seek out those who might offer encouragement, even if we think no one can relate to our experience.

We may not understand one another's particular spiritual expedition, but as disciples, we share the same joy and promise and road. And most likely, similar disappointments. All disciples become our traveling companions on our path to the kingdom of God, winding, yet wending, and one in heart. Each heart holds a story, a call, a commitment, a history, and perhaps a struggle that has shaped our life and brought us together. No injury on the road is easy; however, if we appreciate delays, momentary distractions can bring insight, rather than take us away from our path and disrupt our journey.

When the disciples gathered after Jesus's death, they must have wondered if what they experienced had been real. How had everything gone so wrong? Only days earlier, the whole city had hailed Jesus as king. Then one of their own betrayed him, and now they feared for their lives. What would happen if someone recognized them as his followers?

It is hard to believe the apostles could ever have been afraid. Weren't they the bedrock of the Church? They had actually met Jesus, *knew* Jesus, but they hid out after the crucifixion, afraid someone might associate them with Jesus. Did they forget all they had seen and heard? Miracle after miracle seemed to have vanished from their minds, but then Jesus came back, appeared to them in the upper room, and they remembered.

Jesus didn't just bring a message; he was the message. Jesus was incarnate. He embodied God. Jesus showed us God in how he lived, who he loved, and how he died.

As our journey changes us, we have the power to change those around us, who can then change the lives of others. Two thousand years later, the pattern remains as generation after generation of disciples continues to imitate Jesus. The message of resurrection lives on. What fueled the faith of the disciples after Jesus ascended? How long did they wonder what to do before they realized it was now up to them? How did they first begin to share all that Jesus had taught them? And how did they maintain their faithfulness year after year?

We share the same challenges. How will we carry on the faith that has been handed on to us? This is the question we answer each day. We remain faithful to our path, our call as disciples, and the

Church of our baptism. We build God's kingdom. This is how we maintain faithfulness.

- What does faithfulness mean to you?
- When do you feel most discouraged?
- What helps you maintain faithfulness?

Going Forth

It is hard to experience Good Friday when all we want is Easter Sunday, but that is the "now and the not yet" between earth and heaven. We don't go looking for fatigue, frustration, fear, or malaise, but even potholes can strengthen our faith and commitment. Or at least our ability to strategize! Our task is to remain faithful, no matter the doubt we encounter. This is how we stay committed to our path, the Church, and our lives as disciples.

Talk with someone who models faithfulness for you.
Ask their help to get you there.

Concluding Prayer

Ever sustaining God,
we trust you to make a way,
when we see no way.

Help us remain faithful,
amid struggle and challenge.

May we find hope
when we are weary
and look to you.

Amen +

Chapter 8

A Healing Heart

The healing process begins as we identify our woundedness.

It's rare to get through life without being wounded in some way. People die, relationships end, and dreams shatter. Woundedness is part of our human condition. Someone we have trusted or cared about can hurt us deeply. Family members, friends, and coworkers can let us down, and the very institutions to which we have dedicated our lives can fail us. Grief and hurt are natural, but sometimes our woundedness can get in the way of discovering the holy and seeing the kingdom of God around us.

Pain alerts us when something isn't right in our lives. Pain calls attention to those parts of ourselves that are hurting and in need of healing. Emotional, relational, and spiritual pain can draw our attention inward to our heart. Too much inward attention can isolate us into tunnel vision, and constant inner pain may become depression. We need to pay attention to our pain, but we also need to find ways to alleviate the cause of our pain, so it does not do us further harm. A significant first step might be simply sharing our pain with someone we trust.

Seeing beyond our pain is hard, but when we recognize our woundedness and suffering, healing can begin. Naming our pain might feel more distressing than our initial hurt, but it is essential to any healing process. Identifying our pain can open the door to healing.

Much suffering finds its roots in love. Suffering and joy can stretch our heart, teach us to love more deeply, and help us better understand those who suffer. Suffering is a hard cross to bear—just ask Jesus. Jesus stretched his heart beyond breaking, even beyond death, to embrace the entire world. This kind of love is redemptive suffering, a suffering that forms us to recognize the suffering of others in the world. Redemptive suffering is the suffering found in the cross and at the core of the paschal mystery, Christ's passion, death, and resurrection.

Redemptive suffering requires us to empty ourselves, so that we can embrace the suffering of someone else. That is how Jesus loved. That is the challenge he set for all his disciples. We are to carry a cross, not of wood, but of the heart. While it may not be easy, it can become a grace. Redemptive suffering transforms us while it transforms others and brings healing to our lives. With redemptive suffering, we are able to love more deeply and live more fully in oneness with a suffering world and the suffering of Jesus on the cross.

Disarming Our Hearts

Love is a basic human need, not unlike food, water, shelter, clothing, and sleep. However, we aren't always loved in ways that bring us life, or in the ways we should be loved. Sometimes those closest to us couldn't or can't love us the way we need or deserve because they are wounded. If we have not been loved, we may not know how to receive love, accept others, or trust easily. Any vulnerability becomes an opening for potential harm. So, we build walls to prevent others from knowing us. We create barriers to keep people at a distance and wear anger like armor to protect us. We might avoid intimate relationships, isolate ourselves, turn inward, or self-medicate our pain through alcohol or drugs—all for fear of not being loved, accepted, or cared about.

Self-protection is powerful and instinctive. We arm our hearts, because no one likes to get hurt, but in doing so we may thwart the very love for which we long. We even prevent our love for ourselves from getting through.

Until we disarm our hearts, we are not able to live authentic lives. To disarm means to accept ourselves, our gifts, and our limits. We discard attitudes and prejudices that separate us from others. We counter false expectations within and around us and accept the gift of God's unconditional love. We receive the grace and blessing of being God's beloved. It would not seem to be a hard choice—God's love over isolation—but it can be, especially if our need to protect ourselves overwhelms every other belief we hold.

Wholeness of Healing

Jesus offered holistic healing of body, soul, and spirit, not in a magical way, but in a way to help broken believers grow in their faith. The hemorrhaging woman believed in Jesus so completely and was so desperate for healing, all she wanted to do was touch the hem of Jesus's garment. She most likely would have been content to go home and quietly celebrate her miracle, but Jesus sensed healing had taken place, as we hear in Mark 5:30, and he compelled her to come forward to testify to her faith and healing. Her witness no doubt gave hope to others who then believed they, too, could receive grace and healing.

The Gospel of Mathew offers multiple accounts of healing. A paralyzed man picked up his mat and walked (Matt 9:2–7). Two blind men asked for healing (Matt 9:27–31). A centurion sought healing for his servant, who was not nearby, yet Jesus recognized the soldier's public declaration of faith and healed his servant (Matt 8:10). These acts of care brought healing not only to those in need but also offered hope to all who observed the miracle. We might not directly heal others, but we can be vessels for encouragement and support.

As disciples, we proclaim a faith that belies what we see in front of us. We believe in an empty tomb. The family and friends of Jesus saw him die and live again. What looks like loss can become life. Betrayal led to resurrection. Like many travelers, we may think we don't need a map or will just figure it out as we go. That can work for a while, but we can also miss the best of all God has for us on our journey. If we take a second glance in the dark, the Spirit can help us find life beyond grief. Let us believe.

A Disciple's Life

Jesus disarmed people to where they became God's witnesses in the world. Jesus healed obvious needs, like the blind man, the hemorrhaging woman, and the paralyzed man, but he also healed unseen brokenness—damaged relationships, fear or distrust of God, alienation, and shunning from others. Jesus helped his followers understand their self-worth, renew their lives, and find new faith. He not only healed them but also transformed them.

Think of a time when you felt wounded, hurt by a friend, or unsupported in your ministry.

- What happened?
- How did you listen to your heart?
- What did you learn?
- What grace was present?

A Disciple's Heart

The role of a disciple and the work of ministry is to heal brokenness, foster forgiveness, and inspire wounded people to call others to justice, service, and love. Healing and love are gifts to receive, share, and be shared again. Like Jesus, healing power can go out from all of us. We may not raise the dead, but we can lend a hand of consolation, listen to stories of loneliness, and help others understand themselves as beloved by seeing them for who they are: a child of God.

We have been made in the image and likeness of God, but sometimes we think that isn't enough, that we're not enough. We can get caught up in perfectionism, self-generated chaos, and worry about whether we are liked or respected, good at our job, or replaceable. We forget there is no need to worry. We are more than enough. God loves us unconditionally.

As disciples, we are simply to become who God made us to be. This means we accept who we are—our gifts, as well as our limitations, and believe God instead of circumstances. We can be wounded but still share our gifts with others. We don't need to strategize to be successful or popular. We can believe we have a path with heart. While much of our economy is fueled by people doing everything they can to escape their fears of being incomplete, nothing changes the fact that we are unconditionally loved by God.

We don't earn God's love. All we have to do is accept it. Then we are free to walk our path. Free to look within our heart and love what we see. Free to be a disciple who does not have to be anyone other than who we are—baptized, chosen, and beloved. Accepting ourselves begins a circle of love that flows out into the world and can bring about healing in ways we might never imagine. If we share this awareness with others, we can help disarm and dismantle whatever prevents them from accepting they are loved. And when they do, they can share their love with others, as the cycle of love continues and expands. We can celebrate with a community where all are welcomed, where respect and dignity are encouraged, where bread and wine become flesh and blood, strangers become bonded by their baptismal promises, and love and action can change the world.

Jesus introduced outcasts to a new way of being loved just by loving them. The care and love of Jesus show us how to do the same. Let us announce the good news of the risen Lord to the world. Let us be leaven where hope and strength are failing. Let us create and become communion. Let us be what we receive, the Body of Christ.

- What do you like most about yourself?
- Have you accepted that God loves you unconditionally?
- How do you need to be healed?

Going Forth

Accepting ourselves and God's love is the beginning of all we offer as disciples, but it does not guarantee a life free of pain. At times, ministry and discipleship can feel like a bait and switch. We follow our hearts to service, only to find people are not as grateful or receptive to what we offer as we had hoped. It is easy to get upset and exasperated, but Jesus asks us to allow grace and healing to flow. We do not need to be held captive by bitterness. We are beloved children of God.

Rub oil into your hands and arms.
Think of God's healing love.

Concluding Prayer

Healing God,
we are wounded,
we are guarded,
yet your suffering
brings new life.

Help us to live as your beloved.

Make us whole
in body, mind, and spirit.

And love others to life.

Amen +

Chapter 9

Sharing Your Heart

We sow the seed. God takes care of the rest.

The image of planting seeds holds a deeper meaning for those who have grown up planting gardens, farm fields, or even mowing the lawn, only to mow it again. Living our call to discipleship offers a similar experience. We share the love of Jesus and see what grows. "You are loveable" is one of my favorite seeds to plant and one that is at the root of every message God gives us to share.

We might think we don't have the skills, gifts, training, or talent to contribute to ministry or proclaim the good news, but I believe we do. Our actions, words, welcome, and care all plant seeds, even when we are not aware of doing so. If we are filled with the joy of the Spirit and the fullness of God, how can we NOT plant seeds? Like Jesus, we can minister just by our presence. The passion and fervor of the disciples of Jesus began a way of life that has continued for over two thousand years. This is our legacy. Now it is our turn to invite others into a life of faith.

Jesus valued and loved people in every encounter, and he planted seeds through his sheer being. We may not always see the results of the love we share, but even the seeds that fall on a hard path can become food for birds and other animals. We never know the good we bring. Seeds, soils, and sowers provide a rich lens through which to view life, faith, and ministry. While not every effort thrives, our job is to plant seeds and offer unconditional love. We are farmers and gardeners. We sow the seed. God takes care of the rest.

Soil Conditions

Sometimes soil is rocky and unable to hold moisture. It may lack essential ingredients, or we may not have all the tools we need to help growth flourish. There might not be a support system, caring family, or encouraging faith community to guide and sustain growth. Thorns can grow almost anywhere. Addictions, obsessions, possessions, emotions, or too much of anything can choke seeds. Paths may be packed with seemingly impenetrable soil as defenses prevent opportunities for grace or belief in God's plan. But as gardeners and farmers, we need to have patience as we nurture, look out for thorns, care for what grows, and stay open to new ways of sowing. We need to ask ourselves, what took root and what did not? What grew, and what didn't? Thorns abound, but so does good soil. We need to be on alert to both.

However, our personal woundedness may hamper our ability to plant or tend as we would like. We may have forgotten that seeds and plants are not meant to grow without care. Neither are we. Most likely, we remember when we felt like a hardened path or rocky soil, covered by dusty thorns. Perhaps we were not open or aware of the seeds being planted in us by the caring and nurturing sowers in our lives. And then there are those moments when we are the good soil, the seeds take root, and we become a grace-filled harvest because of their efforts.

What Seeds Are We Planting?

Jesus calls us to love everyone unconditionally with a love that is not earned. Jesus loved people to life, not because of what they could do for him but simply because they were children of God. One of the first declarations in the Book of Genesis tells us we are made in the very image of God (Gen 1:26–27). Somehow soil conditions often fail to nourish the fundamental understanding that we are part of God's field. The ultimate source of human dignity is rooted in the unconditional love of our Creator. In God's field, the seeds of compassion, inclusion, forgiveness, mercy, peace, and joy are never fallow. Although any seed can whither without care or sustenance, our relationship with God can grow in every circumstance. If we can trust and surrender, let God be God, and know we are not, we might see a new path, plant new seeds, or recognize new life before us. Our Creator is faithful in every climate and in all soils.

Jesus sent his disciples to heal the sick, resurrect the dead, and drive out demons. We share that same mission: to heal brokenness, foster forgiveness, and inspire wounded people to love and live again, beyond whatever might have brought doubt, despair, or fear into their lives. We are called to use our hands, voices, and hearts to nurture faith, create pathways for justice, and help others do the same. As disciples, we cooperate with God and support grace as it grows, in whatever soil it might be found. Then we do it again. And again. This is the work of a disciple.

A Disciple's Life

We may require support to stay on our path, be formed in faith, and deepen our understanding of God, but nowhere does it say we are to do it alone. Our need for support makes us human, fallible, and open to mystery. The first thing Jesus did in his ministry was surround himself with a band of imperfect followers who ended up changing the world. How's that for a bumper crop?

Think of a time you planted seeds of goodness, grace, love, or faith.

- What happened?
- How did you listen to your heart?
- What did you learn?
- What grace was present?

A Disciple's Heart

Scripture often describes crowds as watching Jesus. Zacchaeus, the tax collector, climbed a sycamore tree to gain a better view (Luke 19:2–4). Story after story reveals how people changed their lives to follow Jesus, be with him, and learn from him. A water jar abandoned, nets discarded, and careers relinquished—all because of their encounter with Jesus.

People also watch us, perhaps from a distance or without our knowing, but somehow, they connect us with ministry or the Church. What do they see? What seeds are we planting in their hearts? Discipleship is fundamentally relational, and sowing seeds is personal, so it matters how we relate to people who live in a variety of soils and terrain. We need to know ourselves and let others know us. How can we plant seeds if we don't want to get our hands dirty in our own hearts?

Are we approachable and open? Does our demeanor offer invitation or imply an appointment is needed? Do we create opportunities for conversation? Or do we let people know about nurturing water, without actually offering any? We need to know our faith, but also have a glimmer of the attitudes we reflect, how we care, cultivate, and conduct ourselves. Hundreds of people see us before we even meet them. That's part of discipleship. How much growth would we expect from a garden we planted in the spring and then only occasionally looked out the window to see how it was doing? Would we be pleasantly surprised, or would we feel burdened by its need for care?

Gardening and farming are an adventure of nurturing and attentive care, not unlike ministry and discipleship. And both flourish in community. Farmers stay connected all over the country, sharing information and supporting one another. Garden clubs abound and host parties to celebrate the fruit and beauty of their labor. As disciples, we care for soil and plant seeds to help others grow in faith. Then water, sunlight, minerals, and good drainage all do their work.

But we don't just depend on the weather. Farmers have barnyards full of machinery to prepare the soil, keep it healthy, and ensure enough water. Gardeners prune, build structures for plants to climb, water when needed, and check in daily to see how their plants are doing. We can't do everything in a faith community, but it's important to know what we can do and what is needed, so no one withers on the vine or dies in the dirt.

Sometimes we see faith develop in a straight line from seed to sprout. Or we may nurture seeds others have planted. Occasionally, we harvest someone else's toil. And once in a while, we cultivate the soil, plant, rejoice in new fruit, celebrate the crop, and enjoy all the grace in between. Every day we follow our path. We never know what might bear fruit, or when. We might expect good growth on good soil, but faith can also take root unpredictably. Different plants require different types of soil and growing conditions. What seed is best planted where? How much water is too much?

At times, we might feel like we are nothing more than fertilizer or a fallow field, but leaving a field unplanted is vital for growth. It may look bare or unkept, but it is a necessary field. It is a field in recovery. The soil is healing. It is a field in need of a patient farmer. It is not always easy to wait while growth takes place. It is tempting to want to see the fruit of our labors, to prove our "worth" as a minister. But letting go and letting God's time be our guide can help us discern the best ways to use our gifts in God's field. What a gift we have been given! Let us tend it well.

- Who first planted seeds of faith in you?
- What helps you grow in faith?
- What seeds of faith are you planting?

Going Forth

Farmers never really take a day off. They fix machinery, research new equipment, commiserate about growing conditions, and make sure they are prepared when the soil is ready for seed. On Sundays, they might go to church, share a meal with their family or neighbors, and get ready for whatever comes next. Committed, caring, and connecting. Sounds a lot like a disciple.

Put your hands in some dirt. Think about the seeds you sow.

What harvest do you hope to see?

Concluding Prayer

Generous God,
all life flourishes in you.

Help us to nurture,
toil, tend, and heal
any obstacle to your grace.

May all who see us,
see you
and long to grow in faith.

Amen +

Chapter 10

A Steadfast Heart

The worst time to sell is at a loss.

When my mom was dying, our family spent countless hours with her in the hospital and at home with hospice care. Sometime later, my wife, Maggie, was recovering from surgery, and I found myself once again sitting bedside at a hospital. During that time, I realized a significant difference between these two important women in my life: Maggie would be getting better. As I held vigil with my mom before her death, I knew the doctors had done all they could, and my mom would not be with us much longer. Though I felt similar emotions of worry and helplessness at both bedsides, understanding what lay ahead made all the difference as I awaited my mom's approaching death and anticipated Maggie's steady progress back to full health.

In times of healing and dying, we embrace our belief in the resurrection and reign of God. My mom and Maggie were doing just that, as my mom began her journey home to God and Maggie prepared to get back to her path here on earth. While a constant source of grace, the Church is not just an institution, but the way we journey as pilgrims to God's heavenly kingdom. This is our foundation as we serve as disciples in our mission to build the reign of God.

Our love for our Church as a community of believers and the mystical Body of Christ can make it hard to accept the shortcomings and failings of institutional Church leadership in recent decades. We are a pascal people who continue to believe resurrection is always near, even if obscured at times by the view of a fallible Church. So, we trust our heartsight and look for signs of resurrection. We do not know the outcome for an ailing Church, but our steadfast heart continues to point to our path and guide us on our road of discipleship.

When I am uncertain about the future of the Church, I try to trust the Spirit and remember that God is bigger than any building or dogma. During times of healing, dying, and struggle, I remember that millions of Catholics around the globe still embrace our shared mission to build the reign of God. The Church is a living institution, full of disciples just like us, so it evolves, albeit over centuries. Perhaps more slowly than we would prefer. Yet we are all fallible. We need to trust the Holy Spirit is working within those leading the Church, even as we do our best to offer counsel that may or may not be received.

The dream of ecclesial institutional leadership is to enthuse all Catholics to live so much like Jesus that they freely and enthusiastically share their faith, so others would also want to become disciples, foster gospel values, treat everyone with human dignity, realize the importance of family, and promote the common good. It sounds like a tall order, and yet Jesus's first disciples seem to have done just that. Their commitment to healing, goodness, and love took hold in such a way that they continue to be our role models today.

We Are Still Here

There are many reasons why any Catholic disciple might want to leave ministry and possibly the Church. But we are still here. Perhaps we are sitting bedside to a wounded Church, trying to determine when and if healing will begin, but we remain faithful. Sometimes the mystery and grace of our woundedness can expand our ministry. In 2009, my good friend and longtime youth ministry leader Lisa Calderone Stewart was diagnosed with terminal bile duct cancer and told she had six months to live. During that time, she made a conscious decision to frame her last months as a form of ministry by praying and sharing her insights about dying and resurrection.

She posted her reflections on CaringBridge, a global, nonprofit social network website that is dedicated to helping people connect during difficult health journeys. Her writings, titled *Dying to Know You Better*, were profound and filled with faith, heart, and humor. I spoke with her regularly in what became my *Tuesdays with Lisa*, echoing Mitch Albom's *Tuesdays with Morrie*, a memoir where he recounted his professor mentor's gradual decline and death from ALS. My conversations with Lisa each Tuesday were grace-filled and sacramental. She knew resurrection was coming; she embraced it and helped others learn from her entrance into death. What a witness to life!

At times, we may feel marginalized in the Church we love, but we are not abandoned by Jesus. Jesus is with us in any cast aside crucible we might experience, as he was with all those who sought his healing and reached out to him: believers, nonbelievers, the ostracized, and everyone who felt banished from human regard. He loved those who denied they knew him when he needed them most. Jesus created a healing community that changed the world. He exemplified how to bring truth to power and find life beyond disillusionment and despair. We can too.

It is not easy to stand in the truth without support, but we have a savior, who is with us each day, at our bedside and at our workbench, guiding our spirit in love. Jesus had shared with his disciples about how to live after he was gone, but they still must have felt overwhelmed as they experienced hope, disaster, disillusionment, and triumphant victory, sometimes within days of each other. At times we might feel lost in our ministry or find ourselves in a Church different from that which first drew our hearts, but we have a powerful example in the first disciples. They saw all they had believed ripped apart before them, then restored in the resurrection. They came to know anything could become right again. Living the resurrection is our inheritance as disciples. Let us rejoice and believe and celebrate with heart! It is our legacy.

A Disciple's Life

An explosion of ministry and parishioner involvement has taken place since the Second Vatican Council, even if it can feel like the Church is standing still, going backward, or at times, less empowered than ever before. It's easy to feel constrained, but the Church can't take away the unique gifts God has given us or remove the path beating within our heart. We are still disciples.

Think of a time when you struggled with steadfast faithfulness.

- What happened?
- How did you listen to your heart?
- What did you learn?
- What grace was present?

A Disciple's Heart

Jesus opened the hearts of his disciples to the deepest realities of life and modeled what it means to truly live, love completely, and be genuinely free. Those who suffer are also on a journey of deep reality, but it is one of pain, death, loneliness, brokenness, and woundedness in what can appear to be an unjust or unresponsive Church. But the darkness doesn't have to win; we can hold on with a steadfast heart of faith. This is the life of a disciple.

Throughout my vigil and days at bedside, I felt fervently faithful to my hopes for wholeness and healing, however events of sickness and death might unfold. Steadfast faithfulness embraces both healing and dying and every doubt of anxiety in between. Our days, weeks, months, and years are filled with moments where we sit with, pray for, wait, worry, and seek support from family and friends as we stay engaged in the process of being Church. It takes time, commitment, and sometimes every ounce of energy we have, but it is worth every effort because we ARE the Church.

It's like the stock market. If you have no money invested, you might not notice or care if markets go awry. But some people have lost their livelihoods and their lives when markets crashed. Likewise, many of us have invested a lifetime in the Church and may be tempted to flee when the outlook seems bleak. However, stock market wisdom remains; the worst time to sell is at a loss.

I've been uncertain if the Church is healing or dying, but I have come to realize my actions and decisions during hard times testify to all that is alive in my disciple's heart during good times. When my path is difficult, I can still support other grieving or struggling disciples and share resiliency in the face of adversity. Not everyone who responds to their inner call may know what or why they believe as Catholics. They might have just grown up "being Catholic," but somehow, they sense there is more to be found. They realize that for Catholics, faith is in the details, even if they are not sure how they all fit together. Time at bedside is when we can realize what we hold in common with others who are committed to building the kingdom of God. These are our travel companions for the long haul.

Most people are tired after cleaning up the church after Midnight Mass, only to come back to lead music at 7:00 a.m. It's not always easy to spend time with fifty-two teens for five days and nights on a bus, no matter the depth of our passion for young people. Still, ushers, catechists, youth ministers, priests, musicians, maintenance people, and countless unseen servants show up, week after week, year after year. We may not know the outcome of our effort, but our presence is a witness to our steadfast love and service. At bedside and beyond.

- When do you struggle most in your relationship with the Church?
- What would help you thrive as a disciple?
- What is your experience of "sitting bedside" in faith?

Going Forth

We all thrive best when we have what we need to stay on our path, remain true to our spirit, and bear fruit in our ministries. What fuels and keeps faith alive is different for everyone. That is why we must continue to discern our call—our path—and listen to our heart. As steadfast disciples, we can offer an abiding presence to a wounded Church and support tired disciples who are wondering what to do next. And we can pray, at bedside, in our joy and pain, together and apart. Just like all who have followed Jesus since his first disciples. We share one road.

Light a candle and write a word of hope to bring comfort while sitting "at bedside" with the Church.

Concluding Prayer

Abiding God,
you are with us,
even when we do not
know where we are.

Grant us a steadfast heart.

Help us to BE your Church
in good times and in bad.

Amen +

Chapter 11

Holy Hearts

Holiness embraces poetic stillness and prophetic action.

Poets and prophets are codependent in the best sense of the word. Poets bring an "innerness" that defines the purpose of a mission and is essential to any prophetic message. Poets pursue a ministry of "being." Prophets engage in a ministry of "doing." The prophet says, "Don't just sit there, do something!" Meanwhile, the poets and mystics say, "Don't just do something, sit there...." Holiness embraces poetic stillness and prophetic action.

Prophets and poets can seem like contrasting roles, but together they hold fundamental and complementary tenets of discipleship. Prophets have a message for the community. Without a vital communal emphasis, our ministry can become lost in personal gratification or distorted individualism. Poets hold an inner wisdom to help us understand the why behind the message that holds the mission. Without a mission, any message for justice and freedom can become a self-focused crusade or favored advocacy. Disciples are not about individualism, no matter our passion, preference, or insight. Disciples promote the mission of Jesus, support the Body of Christ, and build the kingdom of God. Prophets hold every disciple to accountability. Poets make sure the prophet is on the right track.

A Prophetic Mission

Prophets are often the only voice for those without a voice. A prophet challenges complacency that says, "that's just the way things are." Prophets ask hard questions about why some people are hungry, homeless, and excluded from leadership or particular jobs. Prophets embrace these injustices to let God work through them. Prophecy is branded by speech and embodied in declarations against intolerance and violence: "No!" "Never!" "Never again!" Prophets make God audible. Prophets say no to mediocrity, oppressive silence, world hunger, inequality of all kinds, and a status quo that lets evil thrive.

No one plans to be a prophet, but God gave us gifts in our baptism when we were anointed "priest, prophet, and king." We all have the potential to speak out, but prophets discover an unquenchable fire that compels them to amplify their voice to protect the vulnerable. While the roots of prophecy are found in righteous anger, a prophet's mission is bound to the mission of Jesus and brought to life when we challenge communities to make things right for everyone in God's kingdom. We might not all be "out loud" prophets, but we can all do something. As disciples, we use our gifts with the courage of the Spirit and accept God's charge to do the "right thing" and the "just thing," wherever we can, in all ways we can.

The Cost of Prophecy

If I asked you to name a modern-day prophet, Mahatma Gandhi, Jean Donovan, the Reverend Dr. Martin Luther King Jr., or Sr. Dorothy Stang might come to mind. Beyond all they contributed with their lives, they all hold one thing in common: they were killed for their advocacy, service, and message for justice. There is a cost to being a prophet. Jesus was not crucified because he preached a message of love, joy, and peace, but because he challenged the powerful in society to change how they treated those who were ill, outcast, and unable to care for themselves.

Often the disciples asked Jesus how to gain eternal life or, more directly, wanted to know what they would receive since they had "given up so much" to follow him. But Jesus did not use societal math. He confounded their expectations, caused them to wonder how the "last could be first," and angered all who thought they could buy or bump their way to the front of the line into heaven (Matt 19:16–30).

Prophets are not always popular and don't always blend in well with secular or religious circles. But prophets are committed. They are clear. They use their voice, authority, and platform to care for the common good and protect what others might want to destroy or coopt for personal gain. Prophets are the visible sign of God's invisible love, strength, power, and compassion. We each share in the mission to make God incarnate in all we do, whether we are a prophet or a poet, popular or not. This is the life of a disciple.

Sabbath Living

While poets and prophets express themselves in different ways, they both need to stay connected to God and inside themselves. As do we. One way to make sure our intentions are not pushed aside by busyness or distraction is to keep the Sabbath. Sabbath is not only a day of the week. Sabbath is an attitude attuned to holiness. Sabbath is the essence of time. We embody time but are not besieged by it. Sabbath is a summons to live in the present. Sabbath time opens our hearts to listen for what brings us joy and reminds us of what we love most. That's how we enter into the holiness of Sabbath. To be a poet is to practice Sabbath every day. Sabbath time does not equal minutes, but moments. Poets measure time differently; time takes on a new meaning. God's time versus our time, heavenly time versus earthly time, *kairos* versus *chronos*.

We are a kairos people. *Kairos* is an ancient Greek term that personifies the experience of quality time. Kairos time is when we have not talked with someone for three years, and it is "as if no time has passed." Or we talk for two hours, and it feels like two minutes. We are so caught up in the conversation that we "lose track of time," or time "ceases to exist." Alternatively, if we are somewhere we don't want to be, time can seem to drag. We feel like we have been waiting for over an hour and it is only ten minutes. That is kairos. *Chronos* is time we can quantify. It is sequential time: one minute, one hour. We can control chronos time, or we think we can, until kairos sidles in with an idea that engages us and—where did the time go?

Our culture encourages us to live fast but not deep. Fast living and perpetual busyness can deceive us into a race with productivity. We become blind to all that is not about us as we lose touch with our neighbors, friends, or coworkers who "just don't understand" the priorities we have vying for our time. We calculate where our time is "best spent." Our ministry or work can erode as we become more preoccupied with "winning," even as we lose track of the prize.

Sabbath means we let go of chronos time and immerse ourselves in kairos time. We embrace Shabbat, the Hebrew word for Sabbath and a day of rest in the Jewish faith. Shabbat is a day to cease activity. Sabbath is a time to stop, and really "see" injustice and brokenness around us. Disciples are called to a different clock, a different drum, and a different urgency. We are to live in the present on God's time. It is time well spent.

A Disciple's Life

Being a prophet can lead us to Good Friday and crucifixion, but a poet's heart brings us through death to resurrection. In order to be a prophet or a poet, we must be in touch with the story of Jesus. Jesus has to be real for us, not just a theological construct. Jesus did not theorize as to why God asks us to love; he simply showed his disciples what he meant, stayed connected to God, and shared his love with compassion. The road to God's kingdom is paved with prophetic action and poetic presence. These are the two sides of the coin of discipleship. Let us walk together.

Think of a time when a prophet or a poet impacted your faith or life choice.

- What happened?
- How did you listen to your heart?
- What did you learn?
- What grace was present?

A Disciple's Heart

It is not easy to stand against consumerism or stand up for justice. It is harder to do when we haven't eaten, our spirit is starving, or we have not had proper rest. We might feel too busy for a retreat, prayer, vacation, or a family dinner, until we stop and rest and take time for Shabbat. Sabbath helps us remember God's priorities and realize productivity can include re-creation, creativity, festivity, and delight—time to become filled with the Spirit and find our joy in the Lord.

Together, Sabbath, poets, and prophets help us recognize holiness and become holy disciples. If we don't know who we are on the inside, it is harder to authentically give voice to any truth. Injustice can be overwhelming and heartbreaking, but being attuned to God's presence requires us to live deeply with compassion and become practiced at "not doing," in order to "do" with all our heart. Native Americans refer to compassion as "having a moist heart." A moist heart can readily see suffering and pain, and our tears give witness to the vulnerabilities of injustice and societal sin. Compassion doesn't write off someone with weakness, suffering, or limits but stays alert to offer necessary solidarity and support.

The word *compassion* is comprised of two Latin words: *com*, meaning "with," and *passio*, "to suffer." Together they form the word *compassion*—"to suffer with." Living with compassion is to live the Jesus dream with the whole Body of Christ. Compassion walks the road as one community with one heart. We live and die and suffer *with* one another. Sabbath slows us down to contemplate the questions of the prophet who is thirsty for water, knowledge, or renewal. Are we hospitable to strangers, colleagues, and those starved for conversation or companionship? Do we reach out to friends or family who are sick, isolated, imprisoned, or shunned by society? Do we share our food, clothes, and possessions with those who are without? Do we take time to notice these needs?

During Sabbath, we look inward to find our poet. The poet reminds us it is not enough to do for Jesus, but we must also live in Jesus—heart, mind, and soul. We then look outward with the eyes of a prophet to confront injustice, oppression, and violence. Our holiness is embodied both when we "do something" and when we "sit there."

We might need to "stretch" our holiness to both "do" and "be," as we advocate together to promote justice and truth. Sabbath reminds us that our presence is God's way of being present in the world and our way of being with God. Together, we learn how to "be" with each other and all of creation.

- Who are the prophets in your life? Who are your poets?
- Who are you most of the time—a prophet or a poet?
- How can you "stretch" your holiness?

Going Forth

As disciples, we are to move hearts to action. Prophets curse the darkness. Poets light candles. Jesus built a community of believers to let people know they were not alone in their hunger for meaning, belonging, and justice. We live the ongoing Christmas-

Easter message: light comes into the world, and resurrection overcomes crucifixion. Through this prism of holiness, the light of Christ penetrates all darkness. Let us be a holy prism for others.

Make a list of the people, places, or events that have shown you a "moist heart." Recall how the prophet and poet stirred within you.

Concluding Prayer

Passionate God,
you give us zeal and courage
to compel the world to care.

Help us be still,
to notice you and those
with no voice.

May we hear your message
and share it
whenever we can,
in all ways we can.

Amen +

Chapter 12

Hearts on Fire

How about you be Jesus today?

We are surrounded by a great cloud of witnesses—our Communion of Saints! These are our spiritual ancestors whose lives were such models of discipleship that the Catholic Church decided to honor them so we would never forget how they lived their faith. You might have a family member who is remembered for their love or kindness, cooking, jokes, hospitality, or other attributes. Memories and stories might come to mind each time friends or family gather. "Remember when…," or "I loved how she would…." In a similar way, Catholics prayerfully invoke the names of saints to remember their witness and call on them as fellow pilgrims, as we might ask a friend or neighbor to pray for us.

The Communion of Saints binds us together with all who have gone before us, marked with the sign of faith. They are our community of memory and hope, a holy people touched with the fire of the Spirit, summoned to bring the face of divine compassion to daily life and the great struggles of history. They wrestled with evil and delighted when justice, peace, and healing gained any foothold. They join heaven to earth, and we look to them for their heavenly view, now far beyond our own.

As the world becomes more complex and filled with all that can be unseemly and unsaintly, saints become an intriguing anomaly. Their lives of conviction, purpose, and self-giving contrast with the societal dream of acquisition and self-focus to offer clarity and transparency. Their service and life with God shaped their path and entire existence. This is how holiness becomes incarnate.

Who Is a Saint?

What images or ideas come to mind when you think of a saint? Perhaps someone holy, meek, charitable, and patient? But if you think again, were Paul and Peter patient? Do we hear about their meekness in the Scriptures? What about Joan of Arc, Maximilian Kolbe, or Dorothy Day? Their actions and legacy carry no hint of meekness.

Canonized saints are those whom the Church considers to have achieved salvation, a word derived from the Latin, *salus*, meaning "health" or "wholeness." The *Catechism of the Catholic Church* describes saints as possessing exceptional faithfulness to God and giving fearless witness as a disciple (CCC §828). Saints are disciples who have become complete in God, raised up as examples for all who long for holiness. Their ability to love helps us love. Their sense of mission calls us to action. Saints serve as models of faith and our companions in service.

Saints are examples of self-giving, sacrifice, and sacrament. The whole world can learn from their hardship, dreams, prayer, and love. The Church and the world need saints, those with hearts on fire who radiate God's grace, who care less about personal gain and more about following God's call, who draw us to love and care for the persecuted, starving, and those without homes or family. Saints inspire us with their spirit, devotion, and passion.

Some saints are designated "patrons." These saints are known for special guidance, protection, or care that relates to their path as a disciple. The practice of patron, or "supportive," saints began with the naming of churches being built over the remains of honored disciples, such as Saint Peter's Basilica in Rome and the Cathedral of Saint James in Santiago de Compostela, Spain. Over time, the idea of saintly protection animated the faithful to claim a saint for almost every facet of life.

Some saints were chosen to connect with occupations, illness, sports, struggling faith, youth, elderly, pets, even pizza, or whatever their faith witnessed. The Church also created a sanctoral calendar to help us honor the witness of our holy ancestors and celebrate them all year long. These days usually correlate with their entrance into heaven. St. Anthony the Abbott is the patron of pizza. St. Francis was known for his love for animals, and churches often remember his feast day on October 4 with blessings of animals to carry on his love for all living creatures. Emulating the lives of saints is one way we can build God's reign. Everything we do can point toward God, even blessing a snake!

Holy Witness

While there are special steps to becoming a canonized saint, every disciple can give witness to the holiness of God. These holy witnesses may not be on the sanctoral calendar, but they continue to be heralded for their faith, perseverance, and zeal. You don't have to be perfect—saints were not perfect people—but they are "perfected" people who inspire others to greater faithfulness. The Communion of Saints binds us to their holiness, not as perfectionists but as our examples of moral, spiritual, and compassionate holiness.

Saints are flesh and blood signs and reminders of lives lived well with God. Saints didn't just tell people how to live, they gave witness to their faith with such fervor that others wanted to live like them, not unlike how Jesus inspired his followers. Saints knew both joy and suffering. They found God in their sufferings and transformed their pain into prayer for others. Suffering calls our attention to people who are sick, marginalized, and victims of violence. We are compelled to open our hearts with compassion, empathy, and redemptive suffering to heal a wounded world. We hurt when others hurt.

Saints are part of the deep reality of life in God, a life lived in communion with the visible and invisible saints all around us. The Communion of Saints speaks to the profound relationship that connects the living and the dead to form ONE Church community on earth and in heaven. This bond helps us grow in holiness on earth as we connect more closely with heaven.

A Disciple's Life

We do not always see the saints among us. Yet their holiness guides us as their moral and spiritual witness expand our understanding of Christian life. The more we are surrounded by saints and the saintly, the more we want to reflect their holiness and goodness. Their path influences our path, and we influence others. This is how disciples share in the Communion of Saints.

Think of a time you were personally impacted by someone's faithful witness.

- What happened?
- How did you listen to your heart?
- What did you learn?
- What grace was present?

A Disciple's Heart

Saints have been transformed by God's grace. Their lives might seem ordinary, but they walk an unexpected path, striving to make faith-filled choices. Saints have learned how to live with adversity, find joy on a joyless day, and dream God's dream, alongside anyone who would tell them otherwise. Saints are willing to stand up for all who cannot stand on their own. They know who they are, whose they are, and stay in relationship with God no matter what they encounter. Their consistent integrity became guideposts that kept them on their path all the way to heaven.

Holiness is such a loaded word. While it can conjure up images of silent shrouded figures, gaunt with fasting, and glowing with impossible virtue, holiness is as simple as being attentive to the presence of God. We allow that presence to permeate our daily lives. However, giving of ourselves is not always instinctive. The story is told of a mother making pancakes for her two young sons: Thomas, age 6, and Jude, age 3. As they fight over who gets the first pancake, the mother sees an opportunity for a teachable moment and says, "Jesus would make sure the other person had food before eating himself." After a few moments, Thomas, the six-year-old says, "OK, Jude, how about you be Jesus today?"

How about we all be Jesus today? This is the rally cry of the saints. Saints did not let their personal preferences, failings, or limits get in the way of their desire to be like Jesus. They believed too deeply and were too committed to being a disciple to let anything block their path. Saints show us that real freedom is found when we embrace any perceived confines, listen to our heart, look for the next handhold, and continue on our path. The path is where all saints began their journey.

Our ability to find meaning on our path can help other disciples discover their own pilgrim way. Saints asked how they could care for others and make the world more like the kingdom of God. Disciples answer that question with their lives. We are still in relationship with all who have preceded us in faith. Death is not an end, but a change. We are all connected. We are all in communion together in the Mystical Body of Christ.

The month of November is a time to remember and celebrate our relationship with those who have gone before us, beginning with the Solemnity of All Saints on November 1 and the Commemoration of All the Faithful Departed, or All Souls Day, on November 2. While these days are often observed solemnly in parishes in the United States with special prayers, icon images of saints, and photos of loved ones who have passed, raucous celebrations take place in cemeteries in New Orleans and various parts of the world. Parades, festive grave-site decorations, commemorative food, and even kites of all sizes in Guatemala celebrate the soul's journey to heaven. Together these two days of prayer have come to be known as the *Dia de los Muertos*, or Day of the Dead, a time to remember all our saints, living and dead, carry on their witness, and make it our own. It is a time to tell family stories, talk about friends and loved ones who have died, eat their favorite foods in their memory, prayerfully invoke their names, and celebrate new bonds of the spirit that sometimes become deeper and richer than in life.

Let us continue to celebrate our ancestors in faith. Holy hearts who have paved the way for us. Indefatigable hearts that continue to energize us as we walk our path. Hearts aflame with the Spirit to inspire and hold our feet to the fire of justice, as they guide our hearts to heaven, surrounded by a cloud of witnesses. Disciples of Jesus are never alone as we pray, *All you holy men and women, pray for us.* +

- Who is or has been an uncanonized saint in your life?
- Why do we need saints today?
- How will you be Jesus today?

Going Forth

Saints pay attention to the Spirit and their path, no matter what chaos swirls around them. They all began as believers trying to understand God's call. Reluctant saints, resistant saints, anonymous saints all became a band of pilgrims who are now our traveling companions. The saints all said yes to being Jesus and encouraged others to do the same. Let us follow in their footsteps. Let us step up and step out—with hearts on fire!

Write down the "saints" in your life.
Say their names out loud and pray for them.

Concluding Prayer

Holy God,
you dwell with us and in us.
Ever ancient, ever new.

Surround us with your saints,
in heaven and on earth.

Help us to be Jesus
with hearts on fire.

Amen +

Chapter 13

Following Your Heart

Move toward a preferred, grace-filled future.

Some days we wake up rested and excited to serve others. We are convinced we are helping to build God's reign. Other days, we are weary and wonder if we are making a difference to anyone. Many days we might find ourselves caught in tedium and monotony. Or we adjust to one change, only to have another upend us again. We might feel like we are white water rafting in a series of holding-your-breath rapids, followed by the tranquility of swirling eddies and calm flat water played out over seasons and then years.

At any point, but often later in life, we can find ourselves at the end of a river, as our work years might be coming to an end, either gradually or abruptly. We might feel called to explore a new river or are tired of fighting the current in the river where we find ourselves. Or our raft has been overturned by unexpected forces "going in a different direction." Whether it's a change we chose or one we didn't anticipate, any life change is an opportunity to recalibrate.

Many people work or volunteer in roles that require skills for planning ahead, developing programs, and managing from a broad vision, yet we fail to do the same with our own future. Sometimes we get so busy doing good for others, we don't notice if what drew us to our path is still our true calling. As we reflect on our path, we might discover that what once brought us joy has now become less life-giving. We might be so distracted attending to details and maintaining our path that we don't notice it turned in a new direction. What do we do when the journey we once thought was for a lifetime no longer brings us joy? Get out the compass—again!

Recalibration

If we are feeling lost or uncertain in our lives, it's important to honestly assess whether our path still has heart. Are we still on the "right path," or is it just the "same path"? Why does the path feel like a chore? It can be scary to realize our passion has changed or we don't know how to fix our sense of dis-ease. But that's how we know it is time to recalibrate.

If you find yourself quietly thinking about a new phase in life, but you're not quite ready to leave your current vineyard, recalibration can shine new light on your path, help you plant new seeds, or realize growth has been taking place within or around you without your realizing new life has begun.

We can only imagine what it was like when Peter let go of his fishing business and decided to follow Jesus. And all the questions! How will you make money? When are you coming back? Who will sell the fish? To recalibrate means to make adjustments that allow us to move toward a preferred, grace-filled future. Recalibration honors our past contributions to work or ministry and encourages us to use our gifts to support the reign of God in new ways, with renewed focus and energy. Recalibration provides an opportunity to choose how much we want to work and at what pace. We can consider a new position, retirement, or semiretirement. We can reexamine our occupation or our vocation. Transition can become a life-giving entrance to a new, joy-filled pathway of grace and balance.

External change might include a new role, location, colleagues, hobby, house, or salary. Internally, we might realize we miss being needed, wanted, feeling useful, or growing, although these might be present in new ways. Change can involve different forms of loss as we enter an in-between time of wilderness or an empty zone where there is uncertainty as we find our way to a new beginning. The process of change brings an awareness that some things are ending, but every ending is a new beginning. It is a good time to use our heartsight! We never know what God might have in store.

Transition and Change

Transition takes time. Good Friday was an ending, and Easter was a new beginning, but in between, Holy Saturday was a period of waiting, confusion, and uncertainty as the disciples grappled with "what do we do now?" Recalibration can often be a Holy Saturday experience, but our belief in the paschal mystery remains central to our way forward. Life may change, but the promise of resurrection does not. Christ died, Christ rose, and Christ will come again. This is the amazing mystery of our faith.

Our faith calls us to use our gifts to work for justice, serve those in need, pursue peace, and help build the reign of God. This effort can take place in Church ministry, but it can also take place down other paths: civil service, your own business, a grocery or retail store, coffee shop, or nine-to-five work that allows you to pursue other interests and talents. Who knows what we might discover once we start dreaming and looking around? What seeds of new creation might be taking hold, despite our feelings of chaos? Recalibration can be a good time to reflect on how you have arrived where you are now, and if or how you would like to expand your journey or begin a new adventure.

Whether we retire, change careers, or decide to step back from our current work for a while, it is critical we do something that matters. Failing to find a purpose can lead to depression and a myriad of health issues. Recalibration, retirement, and any transition is a process of discernment that will vary for everyone. It is tempting to think we need to craft a perfect new identity, retirement, or future work environment, but we do not. The purpose of recalibration is to follow God anew and to live with integrity. We will change as our life changes, but recalibration simply helps us become more of who God has made us to be as we open ourselves to God's grace.

A Disciple's Life

Recalibration asks us to embrace transition and change as we continue on God's path for our lives. It is natural to resist change, even good change, and to worry about new challenges, but our goal is to discover a new fullness of spirit within us. The first step of recalibration is to wonder, "what if..." Then we let go and let God.

Think of a time you kept avoiding a decision
but finally made a change in your life.

- What happened?
- How did you listen to your heart?
- What did you learn?
- What grace was present?

A Disciple's Heart

When we are overworked or have spent a long time in a particular field or job, we might start to feel like no one else can do what we do. We can begin to think we are indispensable. Or maybe we derive comfort from knowing what is ahead of us every minute. We could just be afraid. We need to let go of any performance addiction that tells us, "I am good because of the work I do. God loves me because of the work I do." That is not true. God loves us—period. We sometimes think we need to overwork to prove we are worthy of God's love. But God's love alone makes us worthy. When we let God love us, we can live and work and free fall into gratitude.

Recalibration does not ask us to be reckless, but it challenges us to think about what we might want to do differently. What draws your spirit now? What takes energy? What do you anticipate with joy? What makes you weary? What brings you excitement? What would you do if you could do anything? There might be nonnegotiables, such as income, health insurance, and where you need or want to live. But you can also think about where you "most want" to live. How much money do you need for basics in your life? Can you save for a transition? What have you always wanted to do? "What if…."

Recalibration is not a desert to which we are banished, but an ongoing retreat of new discovery to discern where Christ is calling us now or next. Recalibration trusts the Spirit to guide us in new paths of service and enter unexplored chapters of life. Have you wondered about other ministry or types of work? Now is the time to examine a side path or a whole new road. Recalibration is an opportunity to look at our gifts, what we care about most, and how to pass on our wisdom, experience, insight, and passion to the next generation and keep growing. Imagine your greatest dream. Imagine what a new path might look like. Think about what you hope to find along the way.

It can be hard to visualize even a new hairstyle, but recalibration asks us to try. Recalibration can open up a whole new way to receive God's love. Let God love you and help you discover how to tend to any new spiritual needs. Find a community that can provide nourishment or support. Develop a new prayer pattern and take time to reflect on how God has been active throughout your life.

May the Lord bless you with transition and change—if that is what you choose. May grace help you discern how to use your gifts on your current path or a new route. Remember, God has the map. We are not alone. We are part of a great band of pilgrims, who share a heavenly destination. Listen to your pilgrim heart and grab your compass; it's time to recalibrate!

- What do you fear most about any change?
- What would you do if you could do anything?
- How do you feel God calling you to serve today?

Going Forth

Recalibration gives us an opportunity to foster our creativity. Curiosity is the fountain of youth—we can still learn and grow! We can start or restart a new hobby, learn a new language, study something off the beaten path, go somewhere we've always wanted to go. Do something we've always dreamed about doing, even if it's walking down the street to sit in a new coffee shop. Create a "bucket list" and plan how to cross off one item right away. Then think about what's next. What if…?

Draw a potential recalibration map with any new paths, trails, or destinations that come to mind.

Concluding Prayer

Ever faithful God,
you guide us
along right paths.

ALWAYS.

Help us
trust your way
as we live as your disciples

—Not perfect, but present,
and ready to serve.

Amen +

Chapter 14

A Liminal Heart

The space between choice and change

Pilgrims on the Catholic road saw an amazing juxtaposition of time and transition following Vatican II. Those who grew up with the Latin Mass gathered with those who had no knowledge of it. Some parishes embraced folk music and the "new Mass," while other parishes grieved what had been and did little more than change the Mass from Latin to English. Over time, compromises evolved: the early quiet Mass, the choir Mass, the progressive Mass, the family Mass. The dawn of the new millennium brought a shift in ministerial roles, liturgical guidelines, parish lay leadership, and later, the Roman Missal to revise our patterns of prayer once again.

Concurrently, reports of clergy sexual misconduct began to emerge as Catholics broke their silence in a Church renowned for its obedience. Since the first accusations, it is as if the Church has been punched in the stomach over and over in a watershed of mistrust in Church leadership. Parishioners in the pews couldn't believe such behavior had been allowed to fester. Church leaders seemed to share similar disbelief, but they appeared defensive rather than proactively supporting victims and their advocates. Leaders whom the faithful expected would right the wrongs were instead removed for perpetuating access to the most vulnerable.

A time of turmoil set in as many Catholics felt betrayed by the Church they loved, the media sought to uncover further harm, and litigation threatened to upend what was thought to be an unshakable institution. A bunker mentality seemed to take hold as the Church grappled with how to continue its ministry, protect those potentially at risk, and guard against any future failings and accusations. Throughout the turbulence, Catholics craved stability and yearned for an untainted Catholic identity once again.

Liminality

The height of the clergy abuse allegations coincided with an upsurge in people walking away from institutional religion that, along with a rise in nonaffiliated and disengaged Catholics, has changed the Church landscape and affected its communal, institutional, and financial stability—most likely forever. The Church is experiencing an unchosen recalibration. We are in a liminal time, from the Latin word *līmen*, meaning "threshold." It is an uneasy time, as the Church lurches across a new threshold into unknown realities amid difficult circumstances. We are "betwixt and between" in a "now and not yet" state that contrasts heavily with heaven. It's easy to get lost. Liminality is a vulnerable time of uncertainty but also a valuable space between choice and change. We are not who we were, but we can choose to change for the better.

Liminality is central to our Church. Our beginnings of faith took place in a tomb between Good Friday's crucifixion and Easter Sunday. Holy Saturday was a threshold to life beyond the tomb—resurrection! So too, what we do in the tomb can lead to transformation. Do we hunker down and wait? Impose new rules to control the outcome? Or do we let God be God. The hardest part might be to support everyone who is with us in the tomb as we try to find our way out.

The Bunker

When we feel afraid or hurt, our first instinct can be to build a protective bunker as we heal. Bunkers guard against unanticipated dangers that might disrupt our lives. The hope of any Catholic bunker is to defend against threats that might thwart our return to "the way things used to be" before the disruption. Certainty often brings comfort, so it makes sense to think defining our Catholic teaching and tradition beyond question could prevent any future wrongdoing. However, the bunker can also make things worse.

Rigidity can reduce dialogue and create unintended litmus rankings that elevate those who "obey the rules," while inadvertently forgetting that laws are meant to help everyone live together more easily. Doctrine can clarify but also fuel debate about who is acceptable to receive sacraments, serve in leadership, and be included in decisions. While those in the bunker can seem to be doing "everything right," the apostles did not encourage anyone to stay in the confines of the upper room. The Church was founded by the first disciples gaining courage to walk beyond the door.

The Field Hospital

During a papal audience in 2019, Pope Francis referred to the early Church as a "field hospital," as he reflected on the Acts of the Apostles and their care for the weakest and infirm. This image resonated with many Catholics as a welcome contrast to a perceived overemphasis on superfluous Church pageantry and scrupulous rule keeping. Field hospitals are characterized by flexibility, safety, and a nimbleness to respond. A "field hospital Church" urges disciples to move out into the world to the margins where people desperately need care and justice. Spiritual field hospitals have permeable walls that allow for structure but also accept change and adaptation.

While some Catholics think, "if we could just get back to what we were, everything would be better," not all Catholics trust the shelter once offered by the bunker. Field hospital disciples are wounded healers. They have been hurt by the Church but have found healing and wish to help others who experience a similar pain. Wounded healers realize the good of the bunker but know we are not to live in a tomb. Liminality is our path forward. We are a "both/and" Church that values both boundaries and compassion to help the Church heal and move toward resurrection. It is hard to step over any threshold, but we must find ways to do so together. Every Catholic is part of the Church and part of the Body of Christ.

The Volcano

Although the Church can appear to be a stagnant institution or a massive sleeping mountain, I find it to be more of a volcano. Volcanos look like mountains, but deep inside there is molten rock waiting to bubble up over the volcano's caldera to change everything in its wake. Occasionally the volcano erupts, but then goes "back to sleep" until the next eruption. The resurrection formed the first volcano. Throughout Catholic history, we may remember other outbursts: the Reformation, the Council of Trent, the First and Second Vatican Councils. and now, perhaps, the global Synodal Process begun in 2021.

Some eruptions might seem more positive than others, but the image of a volcano is hopeful for a life of discipleship. It means the Spirit is present in the Church. Even if we do not see it spouting fire and rocks, the volcanic core is fluid and active, as is the mission of Jesus. We might struggle with Church teaching or leadership, feeling alone on our journey, but God is still present. The volcano is still alive.

A liminal heart helps us walk through volcanic ash to new beginnings, survive the chaos of eruptions, and tolerate days when the volcano looks dormant. We don't have to build a bunker to survive, we can recalibrate, continue on our path, and use our gifts to help build God's reign in the world in a new way, in a new time. Amazingly, volcanic soil and volcanic ash are very rich in minerals. New plants and flowers thrive after the lava flow has cooled. So can we, even during great transition and change.

A Disciple's Life

It's difficult to step across any threshold without knowing what's on the other side. And yet the Church has stepped forward century after century, beginning with the first disciples. Church history demonstrates that consistency can be a strength, but change does occur, even if it seems to take forever. We might think the Church is an immovable mountain, but it just might be a volcano.

Think of a time you stood at a threshold.

- What happened?
- How did you listen to your heart?
- What did you learn?
- What grace was present?

A Disciple's Heart

As heaven-bound disciples, we may feel that many days are like the long day between Good Friday and Easter Sunday. How do we live as disciples in the tomb of liminality? What do we do when we don't like the Church as it is, but we don't want to leave; when we miss the Church of our youth, but don't know where we fit in now? We don't want to be in the bunker, but we don't know where else to go. How do we cross the threshold when we don't know what lies ahead? As always, we look to Jesus. "What would Jesus do?" Or as the Church would say, (in Latin, of course) *imitatio Christi*, imitate Christ.

Imitatio Christi is our way beyond liminality. Jesus is our guide to make earth more like the kingdom. The first disciples told the stories that were later recorded by their communities. Over time, their collective memory has been distilled to where a word or phrase such as "Wash feet!" can prompt us to remember all sorts of other "Jesus wisdom." I find a "kingdom litany" can help us assess whether we are helping or hindering God's reign. We need to ask ourselves if we are:

Forgiving. The disciples were always trying to quantify what was asked of them. When they asked how often they should forgive, Jesus gave what was probably an unfathomable number in their eyes, seven times seventy. Seven was symbolic of completion and perfection, so its multiplication announced not only a number but also the infinity of forgiveness (Matt 18:22).

Connected. Jesus always encouraged his disciples to stay connected and begged them to stay awake with him on the night of his passion (Matt 26:38). He likened himself to the vine and his followers to the branches, intertwined in love (John 15:4, 9). He sent them out two by two (Mark 6:7). His message was clear: Stay connected. Don't go out alone. Pilgrims are meant to be with God and one another.

Fruitful. Jesus spoke a lot about fruit: Bear fruit. Be patient. Remember the fig tree. Only good trees bear fruit (Matt 7:15, 18–20). We'll know real prophets by their fruit (Luke 13:9). The same is true for us.

Compassionate. Genuine caring is central to Jesus's message. When did we visit you in prison? When were you in need? (Matt 25:37–45). The parabolic answer is we are all deserving of care; it is more than our ticket into heaven. It can be instinctive to look for minimum investment with maximum outcome. Or we can amaze people with our care.

Peaceful. It is hard to believe the disciples could find peace beyond the violence of the crucifixion, but they found no ordinary peace. The peace Jesus gave calmed fear and was unlike anything they could get from the world (John 14:27). It is still ours today.

Joyful. If we live in Jesus, joy will follow. If we stay focused on the Jesus dream, we might find any gaps in our lives filled with joy. Joy has the power to complete us, as we help others find joy (John 15:10–11).

Courageous. If people didn't believe in Jesus before his death, it would be hard to miss how his disciples changed afterward. Fearful, fumbling followers transformed into disciples of courage and conviction. They believed that Jesus was with them always. The resurrection changed everything, for us too; we are never alone (Matt 28:19–20).

Loving. In the end, the evangelization formula Jesus gave his disciples was simple. Love your neighbor. We can hold a ministry position, a theology degree, or any accolade, but how we treat our neighbors is what tells the story of Jesus (John 13:34–35).

Jesus handed on heavenly guidance to his disciples, who handed it on to us, to take root in all we do.

- What delays you from crossing a current threshold?
- When is the Church most life-giving for you? When is it not?
- How could "Jesus wisdom" help you right now?

Going Forth

Our path ahead is not defined, yet we are called to travel with the end in mind. We are disciples of a pilgrim Church, who live in the now and not yet. The ever-changing landscape erupts, sometime daily, but we are safe in God's care to continue our path.

Draw a "Church volcano" as it begins to smoke and erupt.
Write words for what is emerging.

Concluding Prayer

Loving God,
you give us faithful companions
to accompany us
on our pilgrim road.

Help us cross any threshold
with compassion, courage, and hope.

May we always choose you
in the now and not yet.

Amen +

Chapter 15

My Heart

It's the going that's good!

It is said that pilgrims wander with a purpose. For centuries, pilgrims have traveled the world on different routes with varying destinations and goals, but no matter the reason, all were filled with the desire for the quest and felt compelled to set out on the road. Pilgrims begin with a purpose that ends in encounter, but it's the "in-between" that holds so much possibility: the physical journey, the company of travelers, the wonder of each day, and the adventure that lies ahead. The journey changes us.

While I hope the reflections I have shared here are helpful, my greater hope is for this book to be more than just a quick read. Grace can take root in a new way when it is experienced. We can read about the taste of food, but it never replaces trying a new recipe or the delight of eating and sharing a wonderful meal. A feast with good friends or family is different than sitting alone in your car at a drive-through. A fixed destination and purpose are important, but it's not just getting there; it's the going that's good! That's what makes the journey sacred.

Touchstones

Throughout my spiritual journey, I have discovered five touchstones to guide my search for wholeness and holiness. These touchstones help me keep perspective, find my path with heart, and stay on the road to the kingdom of God. I pray the same for you.

My Vocation. I love the Catholic Church. I have chosen to serve the Church in a leadership capacity throughout my entire professional career. But my call did not come from within its institutional structures, nor is my call dependent on the Church affirming or confirming it exists. The Catholic Church is my spiritual home and where I hold my spiritual roots. I am grounded in my local faith community and nurture my relationships with other believers to help bridge the gap between large Church structures and my day-to-day ministry.

As a member of our local parish, my wife, Maggie, and I form engaged couples, guide confirmation candidates, support youth ministry, and participate in adult faith formation opportunities. We are also part of an "inspirational church" gathering we call "The Dinner Club." We have met monthly to share meals, prayer, and faith for over thirty years. The support of my inspirational church energizes me to participate in the institutional Church and reminds me how all parts of the Church sustain and support one another. While the Church is not perfect, its history, ongoing mission, and constancy strengthen my commitment to my own vocation.

The Paschal Mystery. The paschal mystery—Christ's passion, death, and resurrection—is the central mystery of our faith and my life. Like every disciple since the first Twelve, I live with the uncertainties and contradictions of Good Friday and Holy Saturday and savor the exultation when I place my trust in Easter. The Jesus story has become my story, or I try to make it so, as I remember the good, the true, and the beautiful always outweigh the bad, the false, and the ugly.

Catholic social teaching compels me to engage in our world, and our Catholic imagination infuses every aspect of my life. Catholic rites and rituals, sacraments and sacramentals, pilgrimages, processions, and protests for the greater and common good fuel and form me on my path. I am part of a big church. I try to keep my view large, make room for everyone, and help others on their path. It is not always easy, but the reality of the paschal mystery helps me live within the dying and rising of each day.

Truth. I love our Church, but I do not do so without thought or critique. While laws, doctrines, and precepts can appear to take greater emphasis, the essence of all Church teaching is to ensure the nurturing of faith, care for the common good, and foster encounters with Jesus. Thus, genuine obedience can be a good quality. The word "obedience" comes from two Latin words, *ob*, meaning "toward," and *audire*, "to hear." Together, they form the word *obedire*, which lends itself more to dialogue than strict adherence without conversation.

I love the Church enough to enter into conversation, to speak the truth, and to challenge her when I think it is necessary. When we speak truth in mutual respect, we amplify God's Truth. As such, I also listen to others, the Catholic Tradition, and Church teaching, as well as the Spirit moving in the world. In the end, God is bigger than any one of us.

Integrity. I am here for the long haul. I have had to learn to live with imperfect Church leaders and decisions, but I remain committed to my vocation. Despite disgrace, disappointment, struggle, or disagreement, I choose to work for change from within the Church, like poets and prophets whose inward reflection has led to outward action. Poets and prophets strove to prevent injustice, challenge oppressive institutions, and inspire change—redemptive, liberating, lasting, and lifesaving change. I try to do the same.

In a world of brokenness, the gospel calls me to compassion and justice amid incurable disease, ethnic cleansing, hunger, oppression, violence, abandonment, and more; the list is long. I am not blind to fallibility, but I try to confront challenges by discerning the Spirit working through our pope, pastoral leadership, and Church structures. And I do everything I can to live with integrity. I look at what is critical for me. What are the deal-breakers I fear will prevent the reign of God being present in the world? I try to stay aware of what prevents me from moving forward in my ministry or hinders me from being the person God intends. If needed, I make adjustments. Then I keep walking and working with our ever-present God.

Joy. The mystics tell us joy is the sign of the presence of God. I want to be a person of joy! The temptation is when we think if I get this one thing off my plate, my desk, my list, then I will have time for joy. But there is always one more thing, and joy can elude us, even as we long for it. To be surprised by joy is to be open to the presence of God in unexpected places, experiences, and people.

Most importantly, joy needs to be shared. The disciples gathered each week to share their joy and remember all that Jesus had taught them. Those gatherings were sacramental. Today, our conversations with friends—feasting, dining, praying, walking—and even alone time can all be sacramental and lead to joy. It is important to live with joy, learn to recognize it, and seek it out. Life can change abruptly, and suddenly you are recalibrating and looking for your next handhold. Joy is a great compass!

A Disciple's Life

Like all sacred travel, we never travel alone. We are connected across time and place to other pilgrims—past, present, and future—within our Communion of Saints. These are our trailblazers who have gone before us in faith and left markings and objects for future pilgrims: sacraments and symbols, images and stories that guide us on a trail, mountain, or spiritual quest. We have a heritage of holiness in our journey. Let us continue to carry it forward. It's our turn!

Think of a time you shared your faith with someone.

- What happened?
- How did you listen to your heart?
- What did you learn?
- What grace was present?

A Disciple's Heart

Christianity was a lifestyle before it was a belief system. Faith practices are actions that can form a Christian way of life to sustain our path with heart. These are my "pilgrim guideposts," that keep me on the trail, guide my exploration, and echo many of the themes in this book. Enjoy the journey!

Offer Hospitality. The McCartys have long welcomed people into our home to share food, stories, and conversation at our table. Hospitality is anchored in Scripture and became essential for ancient pilgrims who sought out homes marked with symbols that identified where pilgrims were invited to receive food, rest, and welcome. The scallop shell in Spain, the heart on journeys to Rome, and palm branches for Jerusalem all alerted travelers to safe shelter. Hospitality is our way of entertaining angels unaware.

Keep the Sabbath. It is hard work to "not work." But it is important to find a rhythm to each day that honors genuine rest and creates space in your home and lives for rejuvenating rest, family, and friends. It's not always easy, but Maggie and I have made it a priority, especially now that we have grandchildren. Sabbath is time to relax in God and savor each moment, not just on Sunday but every day.

Participate in a Faith Community. While parishes bring us together in a variety of ways, they might not meet all our spiritual needs, or we might not be able to be present as much as we would like due to varying schedules and lifestyles of work and home. My inspirational "Dinner Club" came together with intention, but at the time, I did not realize how life-sustaining it would become.

Faith-focused book clubs, informal or formal prayer groups, collective acts of justice, faith-sharing groups, and opportunities to learn more about Church and life, beyond the Sunday gathering, can help create a deeper sense of connection around the eucharistic table. If you are overwhelmed with responsibility, often traveling, or feeling isolated and disconnected throughout the week, it's a blessing to have a community where you are missed and welcomed home.

Embrace Your Occupation. Work is one of the ways we express our identity and how we engage with the world, so I try to live my faith as a "ministry in the marketplace." All time then becomes an opportunity to build the kingdom of God. As I balance work with other needs and responsibilities, my vocation can become a generative life of spirit, service, and care—wherever I am.

Treasure Your Journey Companions. My spiritual journey continues to bring me together with terrific people and encounters that have turned into lasting bonds and life-giving gatherings. Maggie and I have our monthly Dinner Club, an occasional "wine and wisdom" gathering of Catholics who feel disconnected from the Church, and our Shadetree Sippers, a band of adventure companions on our street with whom we travel. We also enjoy a network of ministry colleagues whose commitment to Jesus Christ remains lifesaving and life-giving. These relationships have become sacred as we share meals, a passion for life and goodness, and faith on our pilgrim journey.

Engage in Heart Service. Mother Teresa is attributed with saying, "Service is the rent we pay for living on the earth." Service is discipleship in action. Involvement in our local community and outreach efforts expands our heart beyond our ministry and faith community to wherever we are and whenever a moment of need presents itself.

Listen to Stories. Listening to others share stories of God's activity strengthens my faith and provides a rich source of grace. It is equally powerful and challenging to hear from those who minister in settings where oppression, violence, and poverty have become the norm. It is vital to hear the truth about injustice, listen to the marginalized, and allow these stories to shape our lives.

Take Time to Pray. Whether it's a set time of day, a special spot in your home, driving or riding in a car, being alone or with others, it is essential to pray. A regular pattern of prayer strengthens our relationship with God, fosters a deeper awareness of God's presence, and offers daily grace. Scripture or spiritual reading can be helpful, but the goal is to communicate with God intentionally and consistently.

Use Heartsight. Being able to "see" takes practice. When heartsight becomes second nature, grace can abound. But first, we have to look for God's presence to see the reign of God break through. Then, ordinary days become amazing days as we are surrounded by the awe and wonder of God's kingdom unfolding within and around us.

Keep an Attitude of Gratitude. Take every opportunity to recognize the gifts of our Creator and give thanks. At mealtime, before sleep, upon rising, over coffee, when you experience joy or sadness, as things go right or wrong, during encounters with children or grandchildren, and every moment in between. Gratitude can become our breath. In with thanks, out with praise. Gratitude shapes our attitude.

- What do you hope for most on your pilgrim path?
- What faith practices are most helpful on your road?
- What excites you about your journey with God?

Going Forth

The metaphors of journey, pilgrimage, and path resonate with my life experiences. Destinations provide direction, purpose, and meaning, but reaching a destination is not as important as setting out. Following our path, and all the grace it holds, helps us become the disciples God intends us to be—not just following along but going somewhere. Let us go with heart!

Name one insight, action, or decision that will bring joy to your journey. Onward!

Concluding Prayer

God of our every step,
you invite us to be
your disciples.

Guide us on our path,
and help us share you
with the world.

May we listen with our heart
to hear your heart
at every crossroad.

Onward!

Amen +